An Analysis of

René Descartes's

Meditations on
First Philosophy

Andreas Vrahimis

Published by Macat International Ltd
24:13 Coda Centre, 189 Munster Road, London SW6 6AW.

Distributed exclusively by Routledge
2 Park Square, Milton Park, Abingdon, Oxon OX14 4RN
711 Third Avenue, New York, NY 10017, USA

Routledge is an imprint of the Taylor & Francis Group, an informa business

www.macat.com
info@macat.com

Cataloguing in Publication Data
A catalogue record for this book is available from the British Library.
Library of Congress Cataloguing-in-Publication Data is available upon request.
Cover illustration: Etienne Gilfillan

ISBN 978-1-912302-97-0 (hardback)
ISBN 978-1-912127-32-0 (paperback)
ISBN 978-1-912281-85-5 (e-book)

Notice

CONTENTS

THE MACAT LIBRARY

The Macat Library is a series of unique academic explorations of seminal works in the humanities and social sciences – books and papers that have had a significant and widely recognised impact on their disciplines. It has been created to serve as much more than just a summary of what lies between the covers of a great book. It illuminates and explores the influences on, ideas of, and impact of that book. Our goal is to offer a learning resource that encourages critical thinking and fosters a better, deeper understanding of important ideas.

Each publication is divided into three Sections: Influences, Ideas, and Impact. Each Section has four Modules. These explore every important facet of the work, and the responses to it.

This Section-Module structure makes a Macat Library book easy to use, but it has another important feature. Because each Macat book is written to the same format, it is possible (and encouraged!) to cross-reference multiple Macat books along the same lines of inquiry or research. This allows the reader to open up interesting interdisciplinary pathways.

To further aid your reading, lists of glossary terms and people mentioned are included at the end of this book (these are indicated by an asterisk [*] throughout) – as well as a list of works cited.

Macat has worked with the University of Cambridge to identify the elements of critical thinking and understand the ways in which six different skills combine to enable effective thinking.
Three allow us to fully understand a problem; three more give us the tools to solve it. Together, these six skills make up the **PACIER** model of critical thinking. They are:

ANALYSIS – understanding how an argument is built
EVALUATION – exploring the strengths and weaknesses of an argument
INTERPRETATION – understanding issues of meaning

CREATIVE THINKING – coming up with new ideas and fresh connections
PROBLEM-SOLVING – producing strong solutions
REASONING – creating strong arguments

To find out more, visit **WWW.MACAT.COM.**

CRITICAL THINKING AND *MEDITATIONS*

Primary critical thinking skill: REASONING
Secondary critical thinking skill: INTERPRETATION

René Descartes's 1641 *Meditations on First Philosophy* is a cornerstone of the history of western thought. One of the most important philosophical texts ever written, it is also a masterclass in the art of critical thinking – specifically when it comes to reasoning and interpretation.

Descartes sought to do nothing less than create a new foundation for the pursuit of knowledge – whether philosophical, scientific, or theological. To that end, he laid out a systematic programme that reinterpreted prior definitions of knowledge, and reasoned out a systematic means of obtaining, verifying, and building on existing human knowledge. To this end, Descartes created a definition of true knowledge as that which is based on things which cannot be called into doubt by radical scepticism. If, he suggests, we can find a belief that cannot be called into doubt, this will provide a solid foundation upon which we can build systematic reasoning. This 'cartesian' method, as it has come to be known, is a blueprint for reasoning that continues to shape the study of philosophy today: a careful weighing of possibilities, searching out solid ground and building on it step by step.

ABOUT THE AUTHOR OF THE ORIGINAL WORK

Born in central France in 1596, **René Descartes** graduated from the University of Poitiers in 1616 with a degree in church and secular law. During a stint as a mercenary in the Dutch army, Descartes met a philosopher, who encouraged him to pursue the discipline. Having seen the results of certain 'radical' writings, Descartes held back some of what he believed were his more 'dangerous' views, fearing censorship and even physical harm. But after he had published *Meditations* critics of his work forced him into exile anyway. In 1649, Descartes left his home in the Netherlands for Sweden, where he was to organize an academy and work as tutor to Queen Christina. He died in Stockholm of pneumonia in 1650.

ABOUT THE AUTHOR OF THE ANALYSIS

Andreas Vrahimis is Honorary Research Fellow at Birkbeck, University of London, UK and teaches at the University of Cyprus. He is the author of *Encounters between Analytic and Continental Philosophy* (Palgrave Macmillan, 2013).

ABOUT MACAT

GREAT WORKS FOR CRITICAL THINKING

Macat is focused on making the ideas of the world's great thinkers accessible and comprehensible to everybody, everywhere, in ways that promote the development of enhanced critical thinking skills.

It works with leading academics from the world's top universities to produce new analyses that focus on the ideas and the impact of the most influential works ever written across a wide variety of academic disciplines. Each of the works that sit at the heart of its growing library is an enduring example of great thinking. But by setting them in context – and looking at the influences that shaped their authors, as well as the responses they provoked – Macat encourages readers to look at these classics and game-changers with fresh eyes. Readers learn to think, engage and challenge their ideas, rather than simply accepting them.

'Macat offers an amazing first-of-its-kind tool for interdisciplinary learning and research. Its focus on works that transformed their disciplines and its rigorous approach, drawing on the world's leading experts and educational institutions, opens up a world-class education to anyone.'

Andreas Schleicher
Director for Education and Skills, Organisation for Economic
Co-operation and Development

'Macat is taking on some of the major challenges in university education … They have drawn together a strong team of active academics who are producing teaching materials that are novel in the breadth of their approach.'

Prof Lord Broers,
former Vice-Chancellor of the University of Cambridge

'The Macat vision is exceptionally exciting. It focuses upon new modes of learning which analyse and explain seminal texts which have profoundly influenced world thinking and so social and economic development. It promotes the kind of critical thinking which is essential for any society and economy. This is the learning of the future.'

Rt Hon Charles Clarke, former UK Secretary of State for Education

'The Macat analyses provide immediate access to the critical conversation surrounding the books that have shaped their respective discipline, which will make them an invaluable resource to all of those, students and teachers, working in the field.'

Professor William Tronzo, University of California at San Diego

WAYS IN TO THE TEXT

KEY POINTS

- René Descartes was born in central France in 1596. He began writing *Meditations* while living in the Netherlands in the late 1630s and died in Sweden in 1650.
- *Meditations* (1641) presents both Descartes's theory that the mind and brain are distinct things and his proof of God's existence.
- Descartes asked questions that opposed long-accepted scientific theories and theological doctrine. Philosophers today continue to try to answer them.

Who Was René Descartes?

René Descartes, the author of *Meditations on First Philosophy* (1641), grew up in a small town in central France. His father, Joachim Descartes, had served in the army and worked as a lawyer and magistrate. His mother, Jeanne Brochard, died a year after Descartes's birth. Along with his brother and sister he was raised by his grandmother.

Descartes spent his formative childhood years at La Flèche, a school recently founded by Jesuits*—an order of Roman Catholic priests. He would later call it one of Europe's most reputable schools. He graduated from the University of Poitiers in 1616, with a degree in Canon and Civil Law (that is, qualified in Church and secular law).

But Descartes did not dive immediately from academia into philosophy. While working as a mercenary in the army of a Dutch prince, he met the natural philosopher—what we might today call a scientist—Isaac Beeckman.* Beeckman continued Descartes's philosophical education and prompted him to write his first treatise, on the subject of music.

As Descartes's philosophy took him further afield, he became worried about censorship. Scientific advances were beginning to challenge traditional beliefs. In skirmishes between the Church and modern scientists, the latter often emerged the worse for wear. Descartes knew what had happened to the astronomer Galileo* when he challenged the long-accepted view that the earth lay at the center of the universe. The Catholic Church branded the Italian astronomer a heretic*—as someone holding beliefs so incompatible with religious teaching as to be criminal. Galileo died following nearly a decade under house arrest.

Descartes feared that the Church would find elements of his natural philosophy equally unwelcome. So he held back some of his more "dangerous" views. Nevertheless, his fears proved justified. After he published *Meditations*, theologians (people engaged in the study of scripture) in the Netherlands—where he was then living—attacked the work and forced him into exile in Sweden. He died there in 1650.

A famous portrait of Descartes depicts him standing on a volume of the Greek philosopher Aristotle's* *Metaphysics*. The visual analogy is apt: an interpretation of Aristotle's philosophy formed the basis for the traditional views that Descartes would come to challenge. Insofar as it posed this challenge, *Meditations* became one of the seminal texts of modern philosophy. In it, Descartes asked questions with which contemporary philosophers still wrestle.

What Does *Meditations on First Philosophy* Say?

More than three and a half centuries after its publication, *Meditations* remains a vital source of new ideas. This is so less because of the specifics of Descartes's answers than because of the questions he posed.

In Descartes's day, modern science was beginning to find answers that upended much established thinking. In the wake of Galileo's well-publicized trial, people began to wonder what other long-held beliefs might be proven false. Such questioning could easily lead to skepticism,* the view that true knowledge of anything remains impossible. Descartes responded by attempting to refute skepticism and establish a firm foundation upon which to ground our knowledge.

Descartes began this project by creating what he calls the "method of doubt." This has become known as the Cartesian* method. It involves suspending belief about everything that cannot be known with absolute certainty. By attempting to doubt everything, Descartes demonstrates that we can discover what bits of knowledge lie beyond doubt.

Descartes's most famous pronunciation—"I think, therefore I am"—demonstrates one of the things of which he believed we could have certain knowledge: our own thought. This phrase actually predates *Meditations*. He first published it in French ("*Je pense, donc je suis*") in 1637. It made its debut in Latin, the language of academia—"*cogito ergo sum*"—three years after the publication of *Meditations*, in his work *Principles of Philosophy*.

Having demonstrated his answer to skepticism—self-knowledge—Descartes turns next in *Meditations* to arguments designed to prove the existence of God. He also introduces the view known as Cartesian dualism*—the idea that mind and body exist as separate substances. Descartes wraps up the treatise by relying on his proof of the existence of God to claim that we cannot be wholly mistaken about the external world we perceive through our senses.

Philosophers continue to debate Descartes's mind–body dualism to this day. It is a controversial idea because, if the mind and body are indeed separate substances, it is difficult to understand how the mind can influence the body, as well as the other way around.

Contemporary readers might be puzzled to find a discussion about the existence of God in the midst of a philosophical treatise. But in Descartes's time, philosophers routinely engaged in such debates. The proof that Descartes provides for the existence of God is an essential step in the move from his position of radical doubt to the point at which he claims to have knowledge about the external world.

Meditations came to be widely read by intellectuals across Europe—many of whom, like Descartes, worked outside the academic establishment. It would be difficult to overstate the work's influence on subsequent generations of philosophers and the development of modern philosophical thought.

Why Does *Meditations on First Philosophy* Matter?

In *Meditations*, Descartes's narrator leads the reader on a methodical journey through his thought processes. He hoped that his rational argument, presented incrementally, would demonstrate the inevitability of his conclusions in a way that could be acceptable even to those who held on to the established views he sought to challenge. He had seen how Galileo had suffered after countering the Church's assertion that the universe revolved around the earth. Descartes wanted to avoid that kind of controversy. But in the end, he could not. A theological polemic—an attack—against Cartesian physics would lead him to leave the Netherlands for Sweden, where he died.

Many of the questions Descartes asked remain fodder for

philosophers today. Although he could not have anticipated the scientific advances that would be made over the centuries, his theory of dualism seems newly relevant to contemporary advances in cognitive science.* We understand much more about the physical brain. Can this lead us to greater knowledge of the mind? Descartes would say no, because the two are separate entities.

Descartes hoped that his writing would reach a wide range of people—academics and non-academics alike. Anyone who has ever wondered where thought comes from, or how we can be sure of the knowledge we hold, will find a sympathetic companion in Descartes's narrator.

SECTION 1
INFLUENCES

MODULE 1
THE AUTHOR AND THE HISTORICAL CONTEXT

KEY POINTS

- *Meditations* is one of the foundational texts of modern philosophy, raising questions with which contemporary philosophy still grapples.

- Descartes wrote *Meditations* after giving up the idea of publishing his work in physics, afraid that it might be condemned as heretical* (as was the work of the astronomer Galileo*).

- In Descartes's day, modern science was beginning to pose a challenge to the Roman Catholic Church and to scholasticism*—the philosophical tradition founded on the work of the ancient Greek philosopher Aristotle.*

Why Read This Text?

In his 1641 work *Meditations on First Philosophy,* René Descartes poses central questions that continue to preoccupy philosophers to this day. A seminal text of modern philosophy, *Meditations* deals in particular with the disciplines of epistemology* (the study of the nature and scope of knowledge) and metaphysics* (the study of the fundamental nature of being, and what we nowadays would name the philosophy of mind).

Descartes wants this work to lay a foundation of certainty for all branches of knowledge. So he questions the degree to which human beings can trust their senses, or even the power of their own minds, in acquiring knowledge. In emphasizing the centrality of epistemology, Descartes introduced many themes that are still

15

> **❝** I have been nourished on letters since my childhood, and because I was convinced that by means of them one could acquire a clear and assured knowledge of everything that is useful in life, I had a tremendous desire to master them. But as soon as I had completed this entire course of study ... I completely changed my mind. For I found myself confounded by so many doubts and errors that it seemed to me I had not gained any profit from my attempt to teach myself, except that more and more I had discovered my ignorance. **❞**
>
> René Descartes, *Discourse on Method*

central to philosophy. These include the problem of the existence of the external world, the existence of other minds, the question of the relation between mind and body, and the issue of personal identity.

To this day, anyone working in philosophy must engage with the ideas Descartes puts forth in this work. Although many of the views discussed by Descartes have been rejected by subsequent philosophers, his *Meditations* itself formulates many of the questions that have led to the rejection of Descartes's views. For example, because Descartes fails to solve the problem conclusively, his introduction of questions regarding the existence of the external world brings it to the foreground of subsequent philosophy.

In *Meditations*, Descartes offers the most significant modern dualist* approach to the philosophy of mind—an account stating that minds and bodies exist as two distinct substances. In this respect, the work remains significant in relation to the interdisciplinary field of cognitive science,* which has emerged in the past 40 years (an "interdisciplinary" field is a field that draws on the aims and methods of different disciplines of study). Descartes's dualism also continues to figure in debates about the philosophy of mind that accompany advances in cognitive science. Philosophers of mind, in part, continue to debate whether or not Cartesian* dualism offers a defensible theory of mind.

Author's Life

Descartes was born on March 31, 1596 in La Haye in central France (later renamed "Descartes" in his honor). His father Joachim Descartes,* a country gentleman who had served in the army, worked as a lawyer and magistrate. He also served as a counselor at the Parlement of Brittany.* His mother, Jeanne Brochard,* died a year after his birth. Descartes, his brother Pierre, and sister Jeanne were left to the care of their grandmother.

As universities became weakened during the sixteenth and seventeenth centuries, the religious order of the Society of Jesus (commonly known as the Jesuits*) rose to prominence as educators. Between 1607 and 1615, Descartes studied at the recently founded Jesuit college of La Flèche. In the first chapter of his partly autobiographical *Discourse on the Method*, he would call it one of Europe's most reputable schools. He studied a syllabus that included grammar, rhetoric (the techniques of persuasive speech), languages (Greek, Hebrew, and Latin), theology (the systematic study of scripture), mathematics, and philosophy. He received his degree in Canon and Civil Law from the University of Poitiers in 1616.

Two years later, Descartes joined the army of Prince Maurice of Nassau* as a mercenary. While serving the prince, he met Isaac Beeckman,* a natural philosopher (the period's equivalent of a scientist) who continued Descartes's scientific education.

Beeckman prompted Descartes to write his first treatise on music, his *Compendium Musicae,* published after his death. He followed this with *Le Monde* (*The World*), a treatise dealing with a range of subjects, from philosophy to the natural sciences, including physics, optics, meteorology, geometry, and even physiology. But Descartes canceled the planned publication of this work in 1633. He had seen Galileo branded a heretic for adopting the view that the earth revolved around the sun. Since Descartes adopted the same position in *Le Monde*, he feared he might suffer a similar fate. After this, Descartes restricted his publications to discussions of epistemology and metaphysics, geometry, optics, and other less "dangerous" subjects.

Descartes began writing *Meditations* in 1636 while living in the Netherlands, publishing the first edition in 1641. But a controversy over his work in the Netherlands forced him to flee to Sweden, where he died an untimely death in 1650.

We should note that Descartes wrote using both the French version of his name and, following the conventions that had governed European intellectual life since the Middle Ages, the Latinized form (Cartesius). This explains why we use "Cartesian" as the adjectival form of his name, as in the Cartesian coordinates* in geometry.

Author's Background

René Descartes lived and wrote during the "Early modern" age,* roughly the early 1500s to the late 1700s, when the rise of modern science began to lead some to doubt the dogmas of the Roman Catholic Church. The Church resisted new scientific discoveries, which would have shown ideas it had traditionally clung to as false. The Church's resistance to the new science was related to its favoring of an earlier revival of Aristotle's philosophy in medieval universities, known as scholasticism.* Modern scientists questioned the scholastic establishment at a price. Descartes saw Galileo condemned as a heretic when he challenged the Church's pre-modern scientific dogma by claiming that the earth moves.

Alongside the Galilean spirit of questioning, thinkers of the

Renaissance—the period following the Middle Ages during which European artists and thinkers turned to Roman and Greek culture to reinvigorate contemporary arts and culture—such as the sixteenth-century French philosopher Michel de Montaigne,* undertook a revival of ancient skepticism.* Descartes's thought fitted into this intellectual and cultural environment by on the one hand seeking to dispel skeptical doubt while on the other trying to give a non-skeptical foundation on which to ground scientific inquiry.

Among Descartes's contemporaries, some could afford to follow their intellectual pursuits as leisurely activities, outside the strict framework of scholastic universities or colleges. Descartes, like many other modern philosophers, was not a professional academic. He thus had a certain degree of freedom, which allowed him to think innovatively. It is arguably this freedom that allowed him to become one of the first truly modern philosophers.

MODULE 2
ACADEMIC CONTEXT

KEY POINTS

- *Meditations* turns modern philosophy toward one of the concerns of the philosophical field of epistemology:* that of certainty in knowledge.

- During Descartes's time, philosophy was still dominated by Aristotelian scholasticism,* which was being undermined by the discoveries of natural science. Parallel to this, a revival of ancient Greek skepticism* had many philosophers harboring doubts about any claim to knowledge.

- Descartes sought to overcome both Aristotelian scholasticism and skepticism.

The Work in its Context

When René Descartes wrote *Meditations on First Philosophy*, philosophy was a broad subject that still encompassed natural science. Up to the nineteenth century, physics would also go by the name of "natural philosophy." In Descartes's time, philosophy would be—as it still is—chiefly concerned with questions about the nature of what there is (metaphysics*), as well as with questions regarding the nature of knowledge (epistemology*).

From antiquity until Descartes's time, philosophers tended to think that metaphysics and epistemology had a hierarchical relationship. One view of philosophy saw it as working systematically through questions of metaphysics, moving on to epistemology, and then to more specific questions such as those posed by the natural sciences. We can think of a philosopher's work as systematic when, for example, he or she employs a consistent method in inquiring

> “ The majority of those aspiring to be philosophers in the last few centuries have blindly followed Aristotle ... Those who have not ... have nevertheless been saturated with his opinions in their youth ... and this has so dominated their outlook that they have been unable to arrive at knowledge of true principles. Although I respect all these thinkers ... I can give a proof of what I say which I do not think any of them will reject, namely that they have all put forward as principles things of which they did not possess perfect knowledge. ”
>
> René Descartes, preface to the French edition of *Principles of Philosophy*

about different fields of knowledge and manages to integrate various fields of inquiry into a coherent whole. Aristotle,* for instance, presents a general account of what causation (the action of causing something) is, which is then applied to the inquiry into causation in different fields of knowledge, from biology to politics and economics. Today this concern for system-building is no longer an essential component of philosophy; it was, however, an important component in the context of Descartes's time, dominated as it was by the Aristotelianism now referred to as scholasticism.

Overview of the Field

Scholasticism was the tradition within which philosophy was taught during the High Middle Ages. As the name "scholasticism" implies, this was an educational movement associated with medieval universities ("schools")—particularly those founded during the late eleventh and twelfth centuries. These universities facilitated the revival of Aristotle in Western philosophy, by translating his work into Latin, mostly from Arabic sources.

Scholars generally consider the thirteenth-century philosopher and theologian Thomas Aquinas* to be the founder of scholasticism. In his work, Aquinas attempted to show that Aristotle's thought was compatible with Christian doctrine. This paved the way for Christian scholars to investigate the topics Aristotle had addressed. These included, among other things, "natural philosophy" (physics, astronomy, and even biology).

After Aquinas, much of Aristotelian scholarship involved reconciling perceived differences between Aristotle's works—written some 300 years before Christ—and the Bible. If, for example, Aristotle seemed to contradict the Bible, then scholasticism would find the appropriate reinterpretation of Aristotle to show that the two texts were in agreement after all.

During the Renaissance* (roughly from the fourteenth to the seventeenth century), the natural philosophical investigations that were made possible by scholasticism progressed further. This gave rise to discoveries that would cast some doubt on Aristotle's doctrines and would in turn result in views that were no longer possible to reconcile with the Bible. The demise of Aristotelianism was further facilitated by a rediscovery of a corpus of Platonic writings, to which Western philosophers had previously had no access.

One philosophical response to this climate of questioning received "knowledge" came in the form of a revival of ancient skepticism. The skeptics of ancient Greece claimed that we cannot know anything with certainty. For example, the ancient Pyrrhonian* skeptics (a school founded in the late second century) exercised what they called the "*epoché*,"* a suspension of judgment regarding anything that cannot be proven as true or false. Renaissance philosophers revisiting this ancient philosophical school considered the claims of both scholasticism and modern science to be equally subject to doubt.

Academic Influences

Descartes presents his ideas as though they are spontaneous creations of a single mind. But not all of them originated with him, as he drew from a number of sources. For example, Descartes's famous philosophical pronouncement "*cogito ergo sum*" ("I think, therefore I am") can also be found in the work of the Christian philosopher Augustine of Hippo* (354–430 C.E.).[1] Similarly, Descartes's argument for the existence of God is a version of the well-known "ontological argument"* put forth by the eleventh-century theologian Anselm[2] (according to which, if God is a perfect being then He must exist, for otherwise He would not be perfect).

Nonetheless, Descartes uses these ideas in very different settings. For example, he placed the *cogito* argument at the center of his work, whereas Augustine of Hippo's discussion of the certainty of self-knowledge remains marginal to his overall enterprise. Similarly, while Anselm makes the argument for the existence of God central to his *Proslogion* (1077–8), Descartes's use of the ontological argument comes only after his own argument involving the notion of "clear and distinct ideas."

Both arguments are used by Descartes to move from knowledge about our own minds to knowledge about the external world—a concern not shared by Anselm or Augustine.

Meditations on First Philosophy is presented in the form of one person's thoughts. Although this is an unusual format for a philosophy text, there are earlier examples of philosophical works written as private meditations. The Roman emperor Marcus Aurelius* kept a diary recording his private thoughts, which was posthumously published as *The Meditations*. The philosopher and theologian Augustine is famous for his *Confessions*, a work of autobiography containing an account of the development of his views on philosophy. Even in Descartes's day, many scholars wrote in the style of "meditations."[3]

Descartes's writing style was influenced by that of his near-contemporary Michel de Montaigne,* whose philosophical *Essais* gave birth to the essay form.[4] Montaigne wrote in his native French rather than the Latin commonly used by intellectuals at the time, partly to reach a wider audience. Descartes followed suit, publishing his *Discourse on the Method of Rightly Conducting One's Reason and of Seeking Truth in the Sciences* in French in 1637.[5]

Montaigne's work was informed by his reading of the works of Sextus Empiricus,* an ancient skeptical philosopher. The ancient Pyrrhonian skeptics proposed the "*epoché*." Montaigne supported the revival of skepticism and used his *Essais*, in part, to cast doubt on various claims to knowledge. Descartes made it one of his chief tasks in *Meditations* to formulate a response to this revival of skepticism. Descartes played skepticism against scholasticism; he tried to show that while the traditional views of the scholastics fell prey to skepticism, his own approach refuted it.

NOTES

1   Augustine of Hippo, *De Civitate Dei*, Book XI, 26.

2   St. Anselm, Archbishop of Canterbury, *Monologion and Proslogion: With the Replies of Gaunilo and Anselm*, trans., with introduction and notes, Thomas Williams (Indianapolis, IN: Hackett Publishing, 1996). See also Lawrence Nolan, "Descartes's Ontological Argument," in *The Stanford Encyclopedia of Philosophy* (Summer 2011), ed. E. N. Zalta, accessed September 10, 2013, http://plato.stanford.edu/archives/sum2011/entries/descartes-ontological/.

3   See Bernard Williams, "Introductory Essay," in René Descartes, *Meditations on First Philosophy: With Selections from the Objections and Replies*, ed. and trans. John Cottingham (Cambridge: Cambridge University Press, 1996), viii–ix. On the meditation style, see James Hill, "Meditating with Descartes," *Richmond Journal of Philosophy* 12 (2006).

4   Michel de Montaigne, *The Complete Essays of Montaigne*, trans. Donald Frame (Stanford, CA: Stanford University Press, 1957).

5   René Descartes, *Discourse on Method, Optics, Geometry and Meteorology*, trans. Paul J. Olscamp (Indianapolis, IN: Bobbs-Merrill, 1965). The original French title is *Discours de la méthode pour bien conduire sa raison, et chercher la vérité dans les sciences*.

MODULE 3
THE PROBLEM

KEY POINTS

- Descartes questions whether there is a way of founding our scientific knowledge of the world on absolute certainty.

- In the face of the empirical* findings of early modern* science (that is, deductions based on observable evidence in the period between the early 1500s and the late 1700s), one could either blindly accept scholastic* dogma (the astronomer Galileo* did not, and the Church condemned him as a heretic*) or develop a general skepticism* about knowledge claims (including those of science).

- Descartes thought that there was a way to answer skepticism that would lay the foundation for modern physics.

Core Question

René Descartes wrote *Meditations on First Philosophy* in a spirit of questioning. In Descartes's time, modern science was making a number of empirical discoveries that disproved earlier traditional conceptions of the world. For example, most medieval thinkers believed that the earth was at the center of the universe. The idea that planets revolved around the sun rather than the earth had been proposed in the second century by the ancient Greek astronomer Aristarchus of Samos*—it did not originate with Galileo. Yet Galileo suffered the consequences of proposing it a thousand years later. Because his discovery was thought to clash with passages of the Bible, the Roman Catholic Church branded him a heretic.

In the wake of the well-publicized debate about Galileo, contemporary thinkers began to wonder: if we can be so wrong

> ❝ Some years ago I was struck by the large number of falsehoods that I had accepted as true in my childhood, and by the highly doubtful nature of the whole edifice that I had subsequently based upon them. I realized that it was necessary, once in the course of my life, to demolish everything completely and start again right from the foundations if I wanted to establish anything at all in the sciences that was stable and likely to last. ❞
>
> René Descartes, *Meditations on First Philosophy*

about something we have believed for so long, what else should we doubt? Can we be certain of any beliefs we have held to be true without having examined them?

In *Meditations,* Descartes examines how we can know anything for certain, whether about the material world or about our own thoughts. Is there anything that cannot be doubted? Is there a clear foundation on which we may base our knowledge of the material world? Descartes aims to defuse skepticism by showing how we can attain certainty in these matters.

The Participants

Epistemology* is the branch of philosophy that considers the nature of knowledge. The majority of pre-Cartesian philosophers (that is, philosophers before Descartes), especially medieval philosophers, do not seem to have paid much attention to the epistemological question regarding certainty, which is central for Descartes.

Neither the ancient Greek philosopher Aristotle,* nor the major figures in the philosophical and educational tradition of scholasticism founded on his works in the eleventh century, considered skepticism a severe threat to their doctrines. For example, although scholasticism's founder, Thomas Aquinas,* discusses some cases of sensory illusion in his work, he does not think such instances prevent us from obtaining knowledge about the world.[1]

Most philosophers before Descartes, both ancient and medieval, had thought that metaphysical* questions—questions about the nature of being—come first. They also thought that epistemology depends on metaphysics. In other words, they prioritized questions regarding *truth* over questions regarding *certainty*.

Epistemology became slightly more prominent with the Renaissance* revival of ancient Pyrrhonian skepticism,* which scrutinizes knowledge claims to reveal their flaws. Pyrrhonian skeptics believed that we could never prove any thesis to be absolutely true or false. In most of Montaigne's* *Essais*, for example, the author discusses various arguments for and against some particular thesis, demonstrating the limitations of both sides. This represents the classic skeptical tactic: abstain from forming an opinion on whatever cannot be known with certainty.

The Contemporary Debate

In *Meditations*, Descartes aims to dispel both skepticism and dogmatism* (the unquestioning acceptance of certain philosophical or religious teachings), thus overcoming the refusal by his contemporaries to accept the new scientific discoveries of the sixteenth and seventeenth centuries because of the challenges they posed to traditional beliefs. He does this by beginning with a crucial epistemological question: what can I know without any possible doubt?

For Descartes, posing such epistemological questions was crucial to his attempt to set all knowledge, and especially the controversial knowledge he thought he had achieved regarding physics, on the solid ground of certainty. If we can find a way of being completely certain of something, then we may base all our subsequent knowledge on this firm ground. In epistemology, this view often goes by the name of "foundationalism."* Furthermore, once we have achieved certainty we can demolish any traditionally established views not based on this certainty, or beliefs that contradict what we have established with certainty. Thus, once the Cartesian* project is followed through, we may be certain, given adequate evidence, that the sun is at the center of the solar system, despite the traditional popularity of the view that the earth is at its center.

NOTES

1   See C. Bolyard, "Medieval Skepticism," in *The Stanford Encyclopedia of Philosophy* (Spring 2013), accessed July 27, 2015, http://plato.stanford.edu/archives/spr2013/entries/skepticism-medieval/.

MODULE 4
THE AUTHOR'S CONTRIBUTION

KEY POINTS

- Descartes replies to skepticism* by taking skepticism to extremes until he finds its limits.

- Descartes's method of doubt leads him to reject basic Aristotelian assumptions (that is, beliefs based on the writing of the Greek philosopher Aristotle*) that had dominated medieval philosophy.

- Though Descartes departs from both skepticism and the philosophical and educational tradition of scholasticism* he does so by partly accepting some of the ideas discussed in both traditions. For example, to dispel skepticism he adopts a skeptical method.

Author's Aims

In his *Meditations on First Philosophy* René Descartes aims to show how one can dispel skeptical doubt and come to find an "Archimedean point"—a hypothetical vantage point from where one can observe objectively—on which to ground absolutely certain knowledge.[1] Shifting paradigms—that is, advocating a very different approach—from all of his predecessors, Descartes thought that absolute certainty would be the foundation of all subsequent knowledge. He considered this certainty to be the root of the tree of knowledge and intended *Meditations* to be a text that would be the firm epistemological* underpinning of his work in natural science, showing how certain knowledge of the material world is possible. In other words, Descartes thought that some basic belief that cannot be questioned might act as a kind of "foundation" on which all

> **❝** Reason now leads me to think that I should hold back my assent from opinions which are not completely certain ... So, for the purpose of rejecting all my opinions, it will be enough if I find in each of them at least some reason for doubt. And to do this I will not need to run through them all individually, which would be an endless task. Once the foundations of a building are undermined, anything built on them collapses of its own accord; so I will go straight for the basic principles on which all my former beliefs rested. **❞**
>
> René Descartes, *Meditations on First Philosophy*

subsequent knowledge could be based. And so, Descartes begins by introducing what he calls the "method of doubt" and moves on to show how certainty may be found in the midst of radical doubt.

It is evident that part of Descartes's intent in publishing *Meditations* was to avoid having his views of physics censored. Rather than launching a direct attack on Aristotelian physics, he tried to pave the way for his own views by writing an abstract treatise on epistemology and metaphysics.*

The distinction between Aristotelian and modern physics has to do with *teloi*. A *telos** is the purpose toward which a thing tends— and which makes a thing what it is. In Aristotelian terms it is not gravity that pulls things downward toward the earth, but a thing's *telos* that moves it toward its natural place. Modern physics does not concern itself with *teleological* explanations (that is, with the description of the *teloi* of things), but, according to Descartes, with mechanical explanations of matter.

Descartes believed that his readers would be more objective in their assessment of his views if he presented them with a series of abstract arguments about mind–body dualism than if he immediately started the discussion with a particular view of matter. In a letter of January 28, 1641 to the French philosopher Marin Mersenne,* he writes, "I may tell you, between ourselves, that these six Meditations contain all the foundations of my Physics. But please do not tell people, for that might make it harder for supporters of Aristotle to approve them. I hope that readers will gradually get used to my principles, and recognize their truth, before they notice that they destroy the principles of Aristotle."

It should be noted that Descartes did not discuss his views on physics in *Meditations*. In his "Preface to the reader" he emphasizes that he wants to clarify his views on the topics of "God and the human mind."[2] His attempt to prove God's existence plays a central role in *Meditations*. His understanding of the human mind is tightly interwoven with this proof. Philosophical discussions of Descartes tend to focus on skepticism, the *cogito* argument, and mind–body dualism. But historians of philosophy see Descartes's theology also as central to his overall project.[3]

Approach

One of the most important ideas put forth by Descartes in this text is its starting point in methodical doubt. This has become known as the Cartesian* method of doubt. It involves suspending any belief that cannot be shown to be indubitable. It is a form of skepticism used as an instrument through which one may reach certainty. For the sake of inquiry, Descartes extends his doubt over received knowledge and, even further, over anything that may be doubted in principle.

Philosophers also call this form of skepticism "methodological skepticism." Methodological skepticism is not a thesis. It is a methodology, a device one employs to achieve an end. When the method bears fruit, a methodological skeptic such as Descartes can overcome his skepticism. The fruit Descartes's method bears turns out to be an answer to skepticism: by methodically doubting everything, we come to find that which cannot be doubted.

It is from this indubitable point that Descartes thinks all subsequent philosophy begins. From there, he expounds on a range of subjects: the nature of the human mind, as he understands it; his attempted proof of God's existence; and the distinction he makes between mind and body. For all of these claims, he relies on the application of methodological skepticism.

Contribution in Context

Descartes strategically employs his "method of doubt" to refute skepticism. Someone skeptical about knowledge of the external world would hold the thesis that the external world is unknowable. But Descartes's methodological skepticism aims to prove that we *can* have knowledge of it. Descartes therefore takes an idea that was in the air at the time (skepticism) and draws it to its extremes. By doing this, he outlines its limitations and tries to show how radical doubt can lead to the discovery of indubitable knowledge.

Along with the Cartesian method of doubt comes the idea that we must ground knowledge in certainty. In contemporary epistemology (the philosophy of the nature of knowledge) this is known as foundationalism.* For Descartes, all knowledge needs to rely on basic beliefs that cannot be doubted. He compared his work to that of an architect choosing solid ground on which to lay the foundations of a building. Descartes built his foundations not simply on the ground of ontology* (the philosophical inquiry into questions regarding being), as most preceding philosophers had done, but rather on a theory of knowledge. In this lies precisely the originality of Descartes's position.

For Descartes, applying his method leads to an indubitable result that can serve as the foundation of all knowledge. Descartes is a rationalist:* he believes that all knowledge can be attained by a deductive process based on this indubitable foundation. Once we have the foundation, Descartes thinks we can deduce from it such things as the proof of God's existence or the proof of the distinction of mind and body on which his physics relies.

This rationalistic understanding of knowledge put forth by Descartes is clearly very different from the empiricist* conception of knowledge that is commonly thought to underlie contemporary science. Empiricist philosophy emphasizes the importance of observation and inductive reasoning—generalizing about laws of nature based on particular observations. In contrast, Cartesian mathematical physics relies on deductive reasoning, which starts with first principles and deducts truth about particulars.

NOTES

1 René Descartes, *Meditations on First Philosophy: With Selections from the Objections and Replies*, ed. and trans. John Cottingham (Cambridge: Cambridge University Press, 1996), 16.

2 Descartes, *Meditations*, 6.

3 See John Cottingham, "Cartesian Dualism: Theology, Metaphysics, and Science," in *The Cambridge Companion to Descartes*, ed. John Cottingham (Cambridge: Cambridge University Press, 1992), 236–57.

SECTION 2
IDEAS

MAIN IDEAS

KEY POINTS

- Descartes treats five central themes in *Meditations*: first, the development of skepticism;* second, the answer to skepticism through self-knowledge; third, arguments for the existence of God; fourth, the distinction between mind and body; and finally, the attempt to prove the existence of the external world.

- According to Descartes, even if I doubt everything, one thing remains indubitable: *"Cogito ergo sum"*—I think, therefore I am.

- Descartes narrates in the first-person a series of thoughts, moving from methodological skepticism to the cogito argument, and then to the attempted proof of the existence of God and the external world.

Key Themes

René Descartes presents his thoughts as a monologue in *Meditations on First Philosophy*. We see the narrator's progress from absolute doubt, through a series of arguments, toward achieving certain knowledge. The first set of arguments concerns the question of the mind's self-knowledge and the unreliability of the sense organs. Descartes argues that the senses cannot be trusted and that the only certainty he can find is the fact that he is a thinking thing. The second argument involves an attempt to prove the existence of God, arguing that he cannot conceive of God's non-existence. On the basis of the proof of God's existence, the text moves toward the distinction of mind and body. Descartes argues that mind and body exist as two radically

> **❝** I shall consider myself as not having hands or eyes, or flesh, or blood or senses, but as falsely believing that I have all these things. I shall stubbornly and firmly persist in this meditation; and, even if it is not in my power to know any truth, I shall at least do what is in my power, that is, resolutely guard against assenting to any falsehoods, so that the deceiver, however powerful and cunning he may be, will be unable to impose on me in the slightest degree. **❞**
>
> René Descartes, *Meditations on First Philosophy*

distinct substances. Finally, Descartes deduces the existence of the external world of matter and the ways in which it may be knowable. Thus, we may discern five themes in the work:

- the development of methodological skepticism
- the answer to skepticism through self-knowledge
- arguments for the existence of God
- the mind–body distinction
- the attempted proof of the existence of the external world through the proof of God's existence.

Exploring the Ideas

Descartes begins the first *Meditation* by developing the Cartesian* method of doubt, step by step. He first observes that his senses can in many cases be sources of deception instead of knowledge.[1] For example, a stick partially submerged in water may appear bent, while in fact it is not. Beyond doubting whether his senses can lead him to certainty, Descartes examines a number of different thought experiments involving the idea that he is being subjected to various forms of deception (often referred to by philosophers as "Cartesian skeptical scenaria"). For example, he wonders whether he might be dreaming, and whether what he thought was waking life may just be a dream: "How often, asleep at night, am I convinced of just such familiar events … As I think about this more carefully, I see plainly that there are never any sure signs by means of which being awake can be distinguished from being asleep."[2]

Descartes even goes as far as to imagine an evil demon bent on deceiving him through illusions.[3] This imagined scenario introduces the possibility that everything he experiences might be an illusion caused by the evil demon. Since this is consistent with what Descartes actually perceives, it leaves all of his beliefs about the external world, about the existence of minds or bodies, open to doubt.

Having reached this position of absolute doubt, Descartes moves on in the second *Meditation* to observe that even if he has been deceived about everything, he is certain that something exists— namely, the thing that is being deceived. In order for me to be deceived, I must exist. So if I think, even if what I am thinking about is just an illusion, I can remain certain that I am thinking. I think, therefore I am—*cogito ergo sum*. This is the foundation of certainty Descartes was seeking.

With the *cogito* argument, I am assured of the existence of my own mind, but the problem of the existence of an external world outside my thoughts remains. I may now be more certain insofar as knowledge of my own mind is concerned, but how can I have the same certainty in my knowledge of the external world of matter?

In the remaining *Meditations*, Descartes attempts to solve this problem. He argues that the existence of a benevolent divine being assures us that we cannot be deceived. Attempting to prove God's existence, he offers a series of arguments. His earliest assertions rely on his concept of "clear and distinct"[4] ideas, which are perceived introspectively. Descartes claims that God is such an idea, and he builds up various arguments that show how God's existence assures him of the existence of the external world. For example, to paraphrase the narrator's argument, I find in myself the idea of God as a perfect and infinite being. Since a finite and imperfect being such as myself could not have caused such an idea, it must have been caused by God.

In case this kind of argument fails, in the fifth *Meditation* Descartes also introduces a version of the "ontological argument"*—the argument that God's perfection implies that he exists (otherwise God would not be perfect). He dedicates the final *Meditation* to clarifying the distinction between mind and body (dualism). This leads to the proof of the existence of the external world through the claim that God is not a deceiver.

Language and Expression

Descartes originally published *Meditations* in Latin and then translated it into French. Latin was the common language of European intellectuals, and was associated with the scholastic* tradition. Descartes's predecessor, the thinker Michel de Montaigne,* had published his *Essais* in his native French, signaling a move away from the scholastic tradition. Descartes followed suit with a translation of the work in French.

Descartes's text employs a particular strategy in setting forth his meditations. The reader is presented with a sequence of thoughts and ideally is meant to put these thoughts under critical scrutiny. If the reader can accept them, then she or he can identify with the narrator and be guided by him from one argument to the next, proceeding through the series of meditations.[5] If the reader cannot accept the thoughts, Descartes has failed to attain his goal.

Descartes's text attempts to leave behind any knowledge acquired from prior authors. The narrator aims at purifying his mind of any trace of "received ideas," holding as true only that which he can bring himself to conceive with certainty. The implication is that, at least ideally, the reader should undergo the same process, perceiving for him or herself the necessity of each step in the narrator's deductive arguments: "I would not urge anyone to read this book except those who are able and willing to meditate seriously with me, and to withdraw their minds from their senses and from all preconceived opinions," he writes.[6] The ideal reader should begin with the "radical doubt" thought experiment and proceed by accepting the narrator's viewpoint only if he or she is certain of it.

Descartes wrote the text in a way that would enable any reader to identify with the narrator.[7] For example, little within the narration gives away its time and place. The only props are almost archetypal: the chair in front of the fireplace on which the narrator sits, the blurry window in which he sees indefinable figures of passers-by, the bed in which he sleeps. Indeed, Descartes has written the book to make a philosophical point: The reader, identifying with the narrator, thinks through the arguments by examining them introspectively.

NOTES

1   René Descartes, *Meditations on First Philosophy: With Selections from the Objections and Replies*, ed. and trans. John Cottingham (Cambridge: Cambridge University Press, 1996), 12–13.

2   Descartes, *Meditations*, 13.

3   Descartes, *Meditations*, 15.

4   Descartes, *Meditations*, 24.

5   For a discussion of Descartes's stylistic innovations in writing philosophy, see Jonathan Rée, *Philosophical Tales: An Essay on Philosophy and Literature* (New York: Methuen, 1987).

6   Descartes, *Meditations*, 8.

7   See, however, Descartes, *Meditations*, 8, where he states that readers who are willing to undergo this process are "few and far between."

MODULE 6
SECONDARY IDEAS

KEY POINTS

- Descartes's dispelling of skeptical* doubt leads to his division between mind *(res cogitans*)* and body *(res extensa*)*, and his attempt to prove God's existence through the notion of "clear and distinct ideas."

- The notion of "clear and distinct ideas" ranks among the most controversial, but also the most influential, parts of Descartes's thought.

- To this day, philosophers still debate the Cartesian* distinction between mind and body.

Other Ideas

According to René Descartes's *Meditations on First Philosophy*, the one thing I can be certain of is that I exist. The search for the indubitable foundation (a foundation beyond doubt) of knowledge leads to self-knowledge, to the "I."

Descartes defines the self as the thinking thing *(res cogitans)*.[1] Whenever there is thought, there is something that thinks the thought. The existence of this "subject" of thought, in Descartes's view, cannot be doubted. This belief that the "I," the self, is the subject of thought that indubitably exists (famously summarized in another of Descartes's works as *cogito ergo sum*) remains one of the core ideas of modern Western philosophy.

Descartes's definition of the self as a thinking being introduces another key Cartesian idea, that of the ontological* distinction between mind *(res cogitans)* and body *(res extensa)*. In making this distinction, Descartes relies on his notion of substance, which

> ❝ When I distinctly see where things come from and where and when they come to me, and when I can connect my perceptions of them with the whole of the rest of my life without a break, then I am quite certain that when I encounter these things I am not asleep but awake. And I ought not to have even the slightest doubt of their reality if, after calling upon all the senses as well as my memory and my intellect in order to check them, I receive no conflicting reports from any of these sources. For from the fact that God is not a deceiver it follows that in cases like these I am completely free from error. ❞
>
> René Descartes, *Meditations on First Philosophy*

diverged from the then-dominant Aristotelian* conception of the term in use by scholastic* philosophers.[2] A substance for Aristotle basically meant a single thing, or entity. For Descartes, substance means a stratum—that is, a layer—of reality, like matter in general in which material things exist permanently. I can know for certain that I am a thinking being, yet it is still doubtful, given methodological skepticism, whether anything other than myself exists.

The problem for Descartes remains: does the external world of matter exist?

For Descartes, the answer to this question requires the refutation of the skeptical scenarios he formulated in the first *Meditation*. It also requires the conclusive rejection of the hypothesis that all my thought may be the product of an evil demon set out to deceive me. Descartes thinks he has shown that there are at least some thoughts about which I cannot be deceived: fundamentally, I cannot be deceived about my existence. But that in itself does not refute the evil demon hypothesis, since I might still be deceived about other things. To disprove the evil demon hypothesis, Descartes thinks he needs to prove the existence of a benevolent God. This leads Descartes to further discussion of mind–body dualism, and finally to his purported demonstration that the external world exists.

It might be difficult now to fathom the implications of Descartes's original mind–body distinction, given how commonplace it is today. It had significant consequences for the development of early modern* science. Dualism* (a way of understanding the world in which, roughly, everything is formed by paired opposites such as "mind" and "body") forms the foundation of Descartes's view that the material world—including our own bodies—works in a purely mechanistic manner.

This means that all its mechanistic (machine-like) functioning can in principle come to be known by science. Furthermore, the mind and its capacity for free will are not ruled by mechanistic natural laws and need not be explained according to them.

Exploring the Ideas
The mind–body distinction leads Descartes to the problem of the existence of the external world. He attempts to solve this through a series of arguments that aim to prove God's existence. First he argues for the existence of God using the notion of "clear and distinct" ideas. We may reconstruct this argument in the following manner:

1. I am an imperfect being.
2. I find in myself the clear and distinct idea of God, a perfect being.
3. The clear and distinct idea of a perfect being must have a cause.
4. Since I am an imperfect being, I could not have caused the idea of a perfect being. (That which is lesser cannot cause that which is greater, and an imperfect being is lesser than a perfect one.)
5. Therefore God exists as the cause of my clear and distinct idea of a perfect being.

Descartes subsequently offers another argument for the existence of God. He bases this argument on the idea that God is the only being capable of causing and preserving a being that has an idea of God, such as myself. Descartes then puts forth a version[3] of the medieval Christian thinker Anselm's* "ontological argument,"*[4] a proof of the existence of God. Descartes's version goes as follows:

1. I have an idea of a supremely perfect being, which possesses all perfections.
2. Existence is a perfection.
3. Thus I cannot conceive of a supremely perfect being that does not exist.
4. Therefore, a supremely perfect being exists.

Descartes goes on to argue that since God is good, He could not be deceiving me, as the evil demon would. With these arguments,[5] Descartes thinks he has established the absolute existence of a thinking ego. He is now ready to consider our knowledge of the external world.

One of the most important notions introduced by Descartes in his theological arguments is that of "clear and distinct ideas." Descartes claims that, on rational examination, he comes to find in himself certain concepts that may be perceived "clearly and distinctly." They are clear because reason can perceive them clearly, and distinct because they are not muddled with other ideas. Such ideas are not acquired through experience but are, rather, innate.* This notion aligns Descartes with the subsequent rationalist* tradition, which would base metaphysical* speculation on the notion of innate ideas.

Overlooked

Although Descartes's thought breaks with scholastic tradition, *Meditations* was written as a text aimed to convince those who still had doubts about the enterprise of modern physics. Some of Descartes's more radical innovations are easy to overlook, as they are often presented in disguise.

One of the most obvious innovations involves Descartes's concept of substance. Descartes argues in *Meditations* that two types of substance exist: mind (*res cogitans*) and extended matter (*res extensa*). Underlying this is Descartes's definition of "substance" (which he poses explicitly only in the subsequent *Principles of Philosophy*) as something that can exist without depending on the existence of another thing. To be precise, Descartes recognizes two types of substance: *God*, an infinite, self-caused substance, and *finite substances* (that is, mind and matter).

God creates these finite substances. But their existence does not depend on each other. This conception of substance plays a crucial role in Descartes's distinction between mind and body, since he argues that a mind could conceivably exist without a body, and a body could conceivably exist without a mind.

Yet Descartes camouflaged this radical idea so thoroughly that even someone as brilliant as his contemporary, the English philosopher Thomas Hobbes,* missed the innovation.[6] When Descartes responded to one of Hobbes's objections, he had to point out that he means something new by the term "substance."[7]

NOTES

1   René Descartes, *Meditations on First Philosophy: With Selections from the Objections and Replies*, ed. and trans. John Cottingham (Cambridge: Cambridge University Press, 1996), 18.

2   See Richard Rorty, *Philosophy and the Mirror of Nature* (Princeton, NJ: Princeton University Press, 2009), 63–5.

3   Descartes, *Meditations*, 45.

4   St. Anselm, Archbishop of Canterbury, *Monologion and Proslogion: With the Replies of Gaunilo and Anselm*, trans., with introduction and notes, Thomas Williams (Indianapolis, IN: Hackett Publishing, 1996).

5   For further discussion of the two arguments, and an introductory defense of Descartes's argument, see Lawrence Nolan, "Descartes's Ontological Argument," in *The Stanford Encyclopedia of Philosophy* (Summer 2011), ed. E. N. Zalta, accessed September 10, 2013, http://plato.stanford.edu/archives/sum2011/entries/descartes-ontological/.

6   Descartes, *Meditations*, 69–70.

7   Descartes, *Meditations*, 70.

MODULE 7
ACHIEVEMENT

KEY POINTS

- Descartes's primary achievement is to have allowed his readers to see they can discuss philosophy in a manner radically different from that which they had inherited from the educational and philosophical tradition of scholasticism.*

- Descartes's views immediately sparked a number of serious discussions among people who had themselves opposed the scholastic establishment of the time in different ways.

- It could be said that in a way Descartes starts philosophy anew, but this does not mean he solved the problems that he posed. However, he certainly began a conversation about them.

Assessing the Argument

As soon as he wrote *Meditations on First Philosophy*, René Descartes sent a first draft of the work to the music theorist and theologian Father Marin Mersenne,* asking him to disseminate it among some of the leading intellectuals of the time. Descartes received a number of objections to the central theses of his book from these intellectuals. In fact, almost all of Descartes's answers to the questions he posed in *Meditations* were immediately challenged. In 1641 he published those challenges, along with his own replies, as *Objections against the Meditations and Replies*.

Many philosophers still debate whether Descartes's replies to the objections are sound. Many have objected to his argument for

> **❝** He is the first man of high philosophic capacity whose outlook is profoundly affected by the new physics and astronomy. While it is true that he retains much of scholasticism, he does not accept foundations laid by predecessors, but endeavours to construct a complete philosophic edifice *de novo*. This had not happened since Aristotle, and is a sign of the new self-confidence that resulted from the progress of science. There is a freshness about his work that is not to be found in any eminent previous philosopher since Plato. **❞**
>
> Bertrand Russell, *History of Western Philosophy*

the existence of God and the way he uses its conclusion to prove the existence of the external world. Even his famous "*cogito ergo sum*," the one thing Descartes thought he had proven with absolute certainty and which forms the basis for the entire book, has been challenged by various philosophers.[1]

Perhaps the greatest achievement in Descartes's text does not lie in the proof of the particular theses he advances. Instead, his most important achievement may have been that he demonstrated a way of approaching the subject of philosophy in a new way. This is particularly evident when one reads *Meditations* alongside the critical discussion that takes place in *Objections and Replies*.

Achievement in Context

Descartes seems to have intended *Meditations* to be used as a textbook at the Sorbonne,* one of the oldest universities in Europe. During the Middle Ages, the Sorbonne had been at the center of the development of scholasticism. In Descartes's day, teachers—not students—used textbooks.[2] He wrote to the Sorbonne's academic community,[3] requesting that they endorse his book. Though he did receive the endorsement, the university did not use *Meditations* as a textbook.

After Descartes published *Meditations*, a controversy erupted in the academic community. A theologian named Gisbert Voetius,* rector of the University of Utrecht, engaged in a debate with the natural philosopher Henricus Regius,* a follower of Descartes who taught at the same institution. The controversy ended badly for Descartes, forcing him to flee from the Netherlands to Sweden, where he soon died.

Despite such difficulties, Descartes's *Meditations* would come to be widely read by intellectuals across Europe. It would be hard to overstate its influence on subsequent philosophy; Descartes was read both by the members of the rationalist* tradition that followed in his footsteps, according to which truth can be achieved only by reasoning, and by the English philosopher John Locke,* who would go on to found the empiricist* tradition (according to which we can arrive at truth only by way of verifiable evidence).

Limitations

Many of Descartes's contemporaries criticized *Meditations*. The English philosopher Thomas Hobbes,* for example, doubts whether in "I think therefore I am" the fact that there is thought requires that there must be a thinking thing. Other critics question whether we can know that what we clearly and distinctly perceive is actually clear and distinct. Critics who address the question of the distinction between mind and body argue that, since we do not fully know the mind, we cannot be certain that the mind does not have a part that is bodily in nature.

In *Objections*, Descartes published arguments that sought to counter the complaints made against his proof of the existence of God. These included reservations about whether we do indeed have a clear and distinct idea of God, as Descartes argues; whether we could not have such an idea without there being a God to create it; and whether it follows from the fact that we can conceive of a perfect being that a perfect being must exist.

One of the aspects of Descartes's text that might seem relevant only to his own time lies in the very attempt to prove the existence of God by way of deductive argument. Although a contemporary reader might be puzzled to find something like this in the middle of a discussion of epistemology,* in Descartes's time it was standard practice for philosophers to engage in such debates. The influential German philosopher Immanuel Kant* would later take a stance against the rationalist tradition's idea that deductive proofs of God's existence should play a central role in philosophical endeavors. That is not to say, of course, that philosophers of religion are not still working on such arguments. But such work has moved to the fringes of philosophy.

Another aspect of Descartes's *Meditations* that is less relevant to our world involves his particular attempt to relate philosophy to scientific knowledge. In focusing on Descartes's philosophical work, it is easy for modern readers to overlook the fact that Descartes's view of science differs from our modern conception of science. His account of science does not rely on experiment and observation. Instead, Descartes saw natural science as a part of mathematics, and as deduced from metaphysical principles.[4]

NOTES

1   See, for instance, Fred Dretske, "Doubts about *Cogito*," *Grazer Philosophische Studien* 84, no. 1 (2012): 1–17.

2   Kurt Smith, "Descartes's Life and Works," in *The Stanford Encyclopedia of Philosophy (Fall 2012)*, ed. E. N. Zalta, accessed July 27, 2015, http://plato.stanford.edu/archives/fall2012/entries/descartes-works/.

3   René Descartes, *Meditations on First Philosophy: With Selections from the Objections and Replies*, ed. and trans. John Cottingham (Cambridge: Cambridge University Press, 1996), 3–6.

4   See Jonathan Rée, *Descartes* (London: Allen Lane, 1974), 20–32.

PLACE IN THE AUTHOR'S WORK

KEY POINTS

- Descartes thought his discussion of certainty would form a foundation on which he could build the rest of scientific knowledge.

- *Meditations* in many ways restates the ideas of Descartes's work Discourse on the Method; together they form the basis of some of the work undertaken in the *Principles of Philosophy.*

- With its acceptance by the Sorbonne,* one of Europe's oldest seats of learning, *Meditations* legitimized—at least temporarily—Descartes's innovation in building a system of knowledge from an absolutely certain starting point.

Positioning

René Descartes published *Meditations on First Philosophy* at what may be seen as the height of his career. It was preceded by an unpublished work on music theory written in 1618, an unfinished work Descartes began writing in 1628 entitled *Rules for the Direction of the Mind,* and scientific treatises on optics, geometry, and meteorology, which Descartes had intended to publish as parts of his book *Le Monde.*

Most importantly, Descartes preceded his *Meditations* with *Discourse on the Method,* a 1637 work that anyone wishing to thoroughly understand his thought should read alongside *Meditations.*

Discourse sets out a number of themes that Descartes would explore four years later in *Meditations.* It is here, for example, that we first find the famous phrase "I think, therefore I am" ("*Je pense donc je suis,*" *Discourse,* IV; also known as "*cogito ergo sum*"), which

> **❝** The whole of philosophy is like a tree. The roots are metaphysics, the trunk is physics, and the branches emerging from the trunk are all the other sciences, which may be reduced to three principal ones, namely medicine, mechanics, and morals. **❞**
>
> René Descartes, *Principles of Philosophy*

afterwards became central to *Meditations*. In his "Preface to the reader," Descartes emphasizes that *Meditations* take up some of the more difficult questions regarding God and the nature of the human mind that he omitted from *Discourse*, because he intended the earlier book to be read by a wider audience.

Integration

The discussions Descartes had about *Meditations*, chief among them his exchange with Princess Elisabeth of Bohemia,* seem to have prompted him to write subsequent works such as the *Principia Philosophiae* (1644).[1]

Principia begins by summing up *Meditations*—although Descartes alters some details. For example, he presents his arguments for the existence of God in reverse order. Then he expands this primarily philosophical outlook into Cartesian* physics. This was Descartes's first attempt to present his thoughts on physics, which are tightly interwoven here with the philosophical views from which he deduced them.

Descartes's definition of matter as *res extensa** led him (wrongly) to reject the existence of a vacuum—a space without matter—as impossible. According to Descartes, the extended material substance is a plenum*—a space completely filled with matter, without any "gaps" or "vacuum spaces" in between. Cartesian physics sees the extended world of matter as composed of infinitely divisible small particles that Descartes calls "corpuscles."*

Though Descartes thought the existence of these corpuscles necessarily followed from his metaphysics* (his philosophical inquiry into the nature of being), other scientists who accepted Descartes's method disagreed with parts of his physics.

In a later treatise on the emotions, *Les Passions de l'âme*, Descartes also extended his outlook into psychology.[2] The passions, according to Descartes, are cases in which bodies interact with minds, with a physical state of a brain being the cause of a mental state. Here Descartes runs into trouble, since the account of mind–body dualism (two-part opposition) he set out in his metaphysics does not seem to allow for such causation.

Descartes saw knowledge as a tree, with the roots laid down by epistemology* (philosophical inquiry into the nature of knowledge) and metaphysics, the trunk growing through physics, leading to the various branches of science (from mechanics to optics, meteorology, morals, physiology, and so on). His own contributions to knowledge range across the tree. Descartes saw them as being unified in this way.

Significance

Meditations offers what Descartes saw as the foundation of all knowledge, and particularly of physics. Yet it avoids mentioning his own work in physics. Descartes, following the astronomer Galileo* and others, based his physics on the idea that the material world could be explained as a kind of mechanism, like a clock. Though the clock might appear like a living being, moving its hands itself, the motion of its hands is really produced by a complex mechanism. Similarly, the mechanistic view of physics, called "mechanical philosophy," proposed that physics explained the mechanisms that lay beneath inanimate matter. This is what Descartes is thinking of when he separates mind and body. The movement of material bodies can be explained in purely mechanical terms. Yet by contrast the mind cannot be explained as a kind of machine.

By starting from such neutral ground in metaphysics and epistemology, Descartes hoped to convince those who might have felt provoked if he had expounded on his own views of natural philosophy. He also hoped to steer clear of the censors. One might argue that Descartes's efforts to avoid censorship led him to develop his innovative philosophical approach. He may have avoided the censors, but theologians in the Netherlands quickly attacked his views. Two academics at the University of Utrecht, Gisbert Voetius* and Cartesian philosopher Henricus Regius,* became embroiled in a debate so heated that Descartes was forced to flee the country.

Although the prestigious Sorbonne University* in Paris endorsed *Meditations* at Descartes's request, the work did not convince many of those who were skeptical of the new science. But his work would soon be taken up by a number of thinkers, whom we may with hindsight place under the banner of "continental rationalism."* The spirit of *Meditations*, addressed as it is to "intelligent men of the world rather than to pupils,"[3] was taken up by philosophers working outside the academic establishments of the time.

NOTES

1   René Descartes, *Principles of Philosophy*, trans. V. R. Miller and R. P. Miller (Dordrecht: D. Reidel, 1983).

2   René Descartes, *The Passions of the Soul*, trans. Stephen H. Voss (Indianapolis, IN: Hackett Publishing, 1989).

3   Bertrand Russell, *History of Western Philosophy* (Oxon: Routledge, 2004), 511.

SECTION 3
IMPACT

THE FIRST RESPONSES

KEY POINTS

- Descartes published *Objections and Replies* along with *Meditations*, thus making critical dialogue regarding his text an integral part of its reception.

- *Meditations* faced objections on all fronts, though perhaps Descartes's attempts to prove the existence of God were most undermined by *Objections*.

- Descartes's *Replies* clarify a lot of the ambiguities in *Meditations*, yet often raise even more debate as to how his thought may be reconstructed so as to answer the *Objections*.

Criticism

René Descartes did not publish *Meditations on First Philosophy* by itself. He took the unusual step of simultaneously publishing a volume called *Objections and Replies to the Meditations*. These included a first set of objections by the Dutch theologian Johannes Caterus,* a second set put together from various authors by the theologian Father Marin Mersenne,* a third set by the famed English philosopher Thomas Hobbes,* a fourth by the theologian and logician Antoine Arnauld,* a fifth by the French philosopher Pierre Gassendi,* another gathered by Mersenne,* and a seventh by the French philosopher, mathematician, and theologian Pierre Bourdin.*[1] Like Descartes himself, most of these figures were also associated with natural science. They shared the broad motivations behind Descartes's project and in most cases they engaged in honest and intellectually stimulating debates with Descartes.

> **❝** From what is said in this Meditation it is clear
> enough that there is no criterion enabling us to
> distinguish our dreams from the waking state and
> from veridical sensations. And hence the images we
> have when we are awake and having sensations are
> not accidents that inhere in external objects, and are
> no proof that any such external object exists at all. So
> if we follow our senses, without exercising our reason
> in any way, we shall be justified in doubting whether
> anything exists. I acknowledge the correctness of
> this Meditation. But since Plato and other ancient
> philosophers discussed this uncertainty in the objects
> of the senses, and since the difficulty of distinguishing
> the waking state from dreams is commonly pointed
> out, I am sorry that Descartes, who is so outstanding
> in the field of original speculations, should be
> publishing this ancient material. **❞**
>
> Thomas Hobbes, *Third Objections*

They criticized a number of different aspects of *Meditations*, the most significant of which are discussed below.

The most serious objections concern Descartes's theology, especially his proof of the existence of God. To this day, most philosophers see these objections as destabilizing Descartes's effort to solve the problem of the existence of the external world by proving the existence of God. Critics have attacked Descartes's arguments for the existence of God from various perspectives. They have also raised various important objections against Descartes's epistemology* and philosophy of mind.

Perhaps the most widely known of the objections is that against the so-called "Cartesian circle"* posed in Arnauld's fourth set of objections.[2]

Descartes had advanced the idea that whatever one clearly and distinctly perceives is true, which is one of the premises of his argument for the existence of God. Arnauld points out that this leads to a vicious circle. Descartes argued first that he had set out to doubt everything, and then that he had discovered in himself the clear and distinct idea of a perfect being, God.

As Arnauld sees it, Descartes's starting point from a position of doubt implies that he should not, at this time, have the clear and distinct idea of God's existence. Yet Descartes proceeds to claim that he discovers the idea in himself. He uses the notion of clear and distinct ideas to prove God's existence, which is meant to safeguard him from deception. Arnauld claims, however, that Descartes's God is needed to safeguard us against being deceived by clear and distinct ideas, and at the same time, clear and distinct ideas are needed for the proof of God's existence. Descartes's reasoning, Arnauld thinks, is thus circular and invalid.

Responses

Descartes maintains that he is open to criticism, but his responses did not always reflect that.

Princess Elisabeth of Bohemia,* with whom he exchanged letters, raised serious objections to the discussion in *Meditations* on the interaction between mind and body. Descartes took those objections seriously—but failed to offer a satisfactory answer.[3] His 1649 work *The Passions of the Soul*, dedicated to Elisabeth, notoriously argues that the human brain's pineal gland is the point at which the mind and the body interact. He thought that the pineal gland was responsible for imagination, sensory perception, memory, and controlling bodily movement. This was seen early on as a slightly arbitrary hypothesis by his critics. The great Dutch philosopher Baruch Spinoza,* for example, in part 5 of his *Ethics* (1677), demolishes Descartes's claims regarding the pineal gland, showing them to be inconsistent with his overall outlook. We now understand enough about human anatomy to know that Descartes was completely mistaken.

Included in Descartes's elaborate responses to his critics is also a response to Arnauld's circularity objection.[4] The response is technical, but can be summarized as follows.

First, Descartes points out that he did not need the existence of God to guarantee the truth of his clear and distinct ideas, as Arnaud objected. Descartes claims that he needs God only to guarantee his "memory" of such ideas.

He then goes on to argue that the existence of the subject of the *cogito* (the "I" of "I think, therefore I am") does not depend on the existence of God. The clear and distinct idea of the *cogito* is immune to the strongest possible doubt and is wholly self-verifying, and does not therefore rely on the existence of God. If we can reach clear and distinct ideas without relying on God's guarantee of their truth, Descartes argues, the allegation of circularity must be dropped.

The *cogito* argument shows that we do not need God to guarantee the truth of clear and distinct ideas, and so the truth of the clear and distinct idea of God does not rest on assuming God's existence.

This response to the circularity objection, as well as his responses to other objections, continue to be studied by philosophers. Many have been regarded as inadequate, leaving questions open for subsequent, often fruitful, examinations of his philosophical arguments.

Conflict and Consensus

In most cases, Descartes responds to objections by clarifying the content of his text. Often he takes the opportunity to elucidate his positions, fortifying them against his critics. But Descartes's attempts to defend his theological views remain among the least convincing parts of the *Replies*. His argument for the existence of the external world depends on his proof of the existence of God. Many subsequent philosophers thought that Descartes was ultimately unable to offer an adequate solution to the problem of the existence of the external world.

The extensive debates between Descartes and his critics did not result in any consensus. The debates went on long after Descartes's death, and even today they are not settled. More generally, the irony is that *Meditations* facilitated the kind of skepticism* that Descartes tried to overcome in the text. If Descartes's arguments for the existence of the external world and our ability to make true claims about it are ultimately just not convincing, we remain stuck at the point of radical doubt from which he started. By doubting all beliefs, Descartes dug himself a hole that (by majority opinion) he did not manage to reason himself out of. As a result, Descartes's legacy is one of radical skepticism, more so than having provided a foundation for the natural sciences. Even today, philosophers argue whether we can ever know whether we are not dreaming, or tricked by an evil demon.

The consensus is, therefore, that Descartes was more successful at formulating profound philosophical problems than with offering persuasive solutions.

NOTES

1   Note that John Cottingham's edition of *Meditations* (63–115) contains only selections from these sets. A complete version may be found in René Descartes, *Meditations, Objections and Replies*, ed. and trans. Roger Ariew and Donald Cress (Indianapolis, IN: Hackett Publishing, 2006).

2   René Descartes, *Meditations on First Philosophy: With Selections from the Objections and Replies*, ed. and trans. John Cottingham (Cambridge: Cambridge University Press, 1996), 102–6.

3   Princess Elisabeth of Bohemia and René Descartes, *The Correspondence Between Princess Elisabeth of Bohemia and René Descartes*, ed. and trans. Lisa Shapiro (Chicago: University of Chicago Press, 2007).

4   For Descartes's response, see Descartes, *Meditations: Objections and Replies*, 93–121.

THE EVOLVING DEBATE

KEY POINTS

- Descartes placed the subject of thought at the center of modern philosophical debates.

- The philosophical tradition that historians came to call "continental rationalism"* (according to which we can arrive at the truth only through reasoning) was born from Descartes's understanding of innate ideas.

- Descartes's work played an important part in shaping the subsequent debate between continental rationalism and British empiricism* (a method of inquiry that emphasized the importance of verifiable evidence in the process of deduction).

Uses and Problems

The legacy left by René Descartes in *Meditations on First Philosophy* and his other works sparked a critical dialogue that has evolved throughout modern philosophy.

The continental rationalist tradition (including the seventeenth-century philosophers Baruch Spinoza* and Gottfried Wilhelm Leibniz*) derived some of its central tenets from Descartes. Spinoza and Leibniz also use notions of innate ideas* (ideas with which we are born) and the concept that true knowledge is to be rationally deduced from basic principles (rather than observation).

But the rationalists* also criticized particular aspects of Cartesian* metaphysics* (that is, Descartes's inquiry into the nature of being).

Spinoza's metaphysics starts with a Cartesian notion of

> **❝**... it must still remain a scandal to philosophy and to the general human reason to be obliged to assume, as an article of mere belief, the existence of things external to ourselves (from which, yet, we derive the whole material of cognition for the internal sense), and not to be able to oppose a satisfactory proof to any one who may call it in question. **❞**
>
> Immanuel Kant, *Critique of Pure Reason*

substance, which we find underlying his division between the thinking substance (*res cogitans**) and material substance (*res extensa**). But Spinoza reworks this into a definition of substance that allows only for God to be considered a substance.

This leads him to the view that "nature" and "God" are interchangeable terms.

Spinoza opposes this to the idea of a personal God that exists outside the cosmos. Leibniz, similarly, though at first attracted to Descartes's mechanistic view of the material world, soon came to criticize the Cartesian definition of matter as being overextended. However, although both Spinoza and Leibniz criticize Descartes's metaphysics, they are also close to Descartes in holding that there exist innate ideas, as well as accepting the idea that philosophical truth is to be deduced from self-evident first principles.

The British empiricist* tradition is commonly seen as fundamentally opposed to the rationalist notion of innate ideas. Although the seventeenth-century English philosopher John Locke* disagreed with some of Descartes's thoughts on innate ideas, Locke's philosophy was partly influenced by Descartes's.[1]

In the next generation of philosophers, one might translate the Anglo-Irish philosopher George Berkeley's* idealism* as the claim that only what Descartes had called the *res cogitans* exists.

The eighteenth-century Scottish philosopher David Hume*
distinguishes between Cartesian methodological skepticism,*
which he calls "antecedent skepticism," and his own, "consequent
skepticism."[2]

The eighteenth-century German philosopher Immanuel
Kant* was scandalized that neither rationalism nor empiricism*
could solve the problem of the existence of the external world
introduced by Descartes. Rejecting various views held by
Descartes, Kant attempted to overcome the disagreement between
the two traditions. In his 1781 *Critique of Pure Reason*, Kant claims
to have refuted a brand of idealism according to which objects in
space and time do not exist.[3]

This brand of idealism is traced by Kant back to Descartes.
Nonetheless, it is clear that the core of Kant's epistemology* tries
to solve the problem of the existence of the external world, a
problem first posed by Descartes. It is, of course, by no means
universally accepted that Kant's philosophy solved this problem.
His successor in the German idealist tradition, G. W. F. Hegel,*
severely criticized the focus on the individual to which the history
of philosophy turned after Descartes.

Schools of Thought

Because of Descartes's conception of innate ideas, philosophers
traditionally consider him to be the founder of modern rationalism,
a philosophical approach founded on the paramount importance
of reasoning. Subsequent rationalists such as Spinoza, Leibniz, and
others, founded their discussions of speculative metaphysics, logic,
and mathematics on the notion of innate ideas—ideas with which
we are born.

Immanuel Kant's critique of rationalist metaphysics in the
eighteenth century halted the development of rationalism. But it
was certainly not the final word in the debate over the existence

of innate ideas. The twentieth century saw various important reworkings of Descartes's views, such as Edmund Husserl's* self-proclaimed, unorthodox Cartesianism, or the various discussions of Descartes's views in the philosophy of mind.

One of the most famous twentieth-century defenses of a type of Cartesian rationalism came from the American philosopher Noam Chomsky.* Chomsky's *Cartesian Linguistics*[4] discusses the thought of Descartes, as well as that of various subsequent continental rationalists, ranging from the writers of the 1660 *Port-Royal Grammar*,* a classic of philosophical inquiry into language, to the nineteenth-century Prussian philosopher Wilhelm von Humboldt.*

Philosophers see Chomsky's own theory of universal grammar* as a type of rationalism. He based it on the idea that all human beings have an innate capacity to learn language. Chomsky traces this idea back to Descartes, and in particular to the idea, which he attributes to Descartes and the seventeenth-century French philosopher Géraud de Cordemoy,* that what separates human beings from animals is the capacity to employ language in a creative manner.

In Current Scholarship

Philosophers continue to rework Descartes's ideas. One of the most famous contemporary examples is twentieth-century American philosopher Hilary Putnam's* brain-in-a-vat thought experiment.[5] This hypothesis reconsiders Descartes's skeptical scenario of the possibility that my perception of reality may be caused by an evil demon attempting to deceive me. In Putnam's scenario, I am a brain in a vat in some laboratory manipulated by a scientist experimenting on it. The deception here is not caused by some supernatural entity, but rather is the result of a physically possible situation. Putnam's scenario has been the subject of much debate among epistemologists, philosophers of language, and philosophers of mind working within the framework of twentieth-century analytic philosophy.

Philosophers in Europe have also sought to build on Descartes's work. Edmund Husserl, one of the founding figures in the phenomenological* movement of the twentieth and twenty-first centuries—an inquiry that emphasizes the nature and role of consciousness and perception—is notable for taking up the word "Cartesian."

In Husserl's *Cartesian Meditations* (1931), based on a series of lectures he gave at Paris's Sorbonne University* in 1929, he reclaims the title "Cartesian" for his own work, seeing in Descartes an early phenomenologist. But while Husserl appropriates the adjective "Cartesian," he also rejects some of the basic tenets associated with Descartes. Instead, Husserl proclaims that in bringing out aspects of Descartes's thought not typically associated with Cartesianism, phenomenology is "neo-Cartesian." Husserl particularly associates Descartes with the phenomenological project of introspectively studying the structures of consciousness.

Subsequent philosophers did not appreciate Husserl's association of phenomenology with Cartesianism. The German philosopher Martin Heidegger,* for example, was one of the twentieth century's most prominently anti-Cartesian philosophers. Arguably, however, it is primarily Husserl's* insistence on seeing phenomenology as Cartesian that Heidegger rejects.

French philosophers influenced by Husserl, such as the existentialist* (an approach founded on the action and thought of the individual) Jean-Paul Sartre,* were friendlier to Husserl's Cartesianism. Sartre's philosophical analyses of consciousness owed much to Husserl's reading of Descartes.

NOTES

1 See John Cottingham, *The Cambridge Companion to Descartes* (Cambridge: Cambridge University Press, 1992), 416.

2 See David Hume, *An Enquiry Concerning Human Understanding and Other Writings*, ed. Stephen Buckle (Cambridge: Cambridge University Press, 2007), section XII.

3 See Derk Pereboom, "Kant's Transcendental Arguments," in *The Stanford Encyclopedia of Philosophy* (Winter 2009), ed. E. N. Zalta, accessed July 26, 2015, http://plato.stanford.edu/archives/win2009/entries/kant-transcendental/.

4 Noam Chomsky, *Cartesian Linguistics: A Chapter in the History of Rationalist Thought* (New York: Harper & Row, 1966).

5 Hilary Putnam, *Reason, Truth and History* (Cambridge: Cambridge University Press, 1981), 5–7.

MODULE 11
IMPACT AND INFLUENCE TODAY

KEY POINTS

- The Cartesian* paradigm (that is, world view) shifted when contemporary philosophy began to challenge the centrality of the individual thinker. Descartes's *Meditations*, however, remains indispensable for anyone wishing to understand this shift.

- *Meditations* is among the most important texts posing the challenge of trying to comprehend the nature of consciousness.

- Philosophers of mind to this day propose various ways in which to understand the nature of consciousness, though each position faces serious problems.

Position

Descartes and his critics set up a number of problems that philosophers are still working on to this day. Whether or not Descartes's attempts at solving those problems were adequate is not as significant as the expression of the problems themselves.

It might be argued that the text's history has been one of ever more vigorous resistance by philosophers. Descartes's immediate successors (the philosophers Baruch Spinoza,* Gottfried Wilhelm Leibniz,* John Locke,* George Berkeley,* and David Hume)* were more willing to go along with basic Cartesian assumptions than were, for example, Immanuel Kant* and his successors, to say nothing of twentieth-century anti-Cartesian philosophical agendas such as those promoted by Ludwig Wittgenstein* and Martin Heidegger.*

> **"**There is a doctrine about the nature and place of minds which is so prevalent among theorists and even among laymen that it deserves to be described as the official theory ... It will be argued here that the central principles of the doctrine are unsound and conflict with the whole body of what we know about minds when we are not speculating about them. The official doctrine, which hails chiefly from Descartes, is something like this. With the doubtful exceptions of idiots and infants in arms every human being has both a body and a mind.**"**
>
> Gilbert Ryle, *The Concept of Mind*

Many of *Meditations'* current applications could not have been anticipated by Descartes. He was, to a large extent, attempting to set an epistemological* foundation relevant to his own and his contemporaries' scientific endeavors. Descartes did attempt to locate the mind in the brain, based on a limited knowledge of anatomy. But he could not have anticipated the relevance of his philosophy of mind to the contemporary development of cognitive science* (the science of cognition—thought), where discussions of the relation of the mind to the brain hold center stage.

Interaction

Contemporary scientists who attempt to explain the workings of the brain still face Descartes's troubling question about mind–brain interaction—with one made of thought, the other of matter. How can our understanding of the physical workings of the brain (for example, knowing that a certain neuron functions in such-and-such a manner) inform us about the workings of the mind (for instance, knowing how a certain thought came about)?

Cartesian dualists challenge the idea of equating the brain and the mind, a thesis that commonly goes under the name of "physicalism." Consider, for example, the following thought experiment developed by the Australian philosopher Frank Jackson.*[1]

Jackson imagines a scientist (call her Mary), who has never before seen colors. She lives in a black-and-white room and investigates the world through a black-and-white monitor. Apart from seeing color, she knows everything else there is to know about color and how it works. Jackson asks whether Mary will learn anything about color that she did not already know if she goes out into the world and sees color first-hand.

Philosophers still debate the answer to this question. The thought experiment hints at the idea that all the objective facts that Mary collects in her room are about physical reality, while what she learns once she leaves the room has to do with the realm of the mind. Descartes would agree with this.

The Continuing Debate

Perhaps the two most influential twentieth-century critics of Descartes are the philosophers Ludwig Wittgenstein and Martin Heidegger. In both of their outlooks we can detect a shift away from the centrality of the individual thinker as the starting point in philosophy. Instead, they emphasize communal (or "intersubjective") starting points.

Someone who follows Descartes might think of philosophy as the armchair activity of a lone thinker. As Wittgenstein points out, such a lone thinker employs the medium of language to describe to himself his own experience. In other words, he presupposes the existence of language, which allows him to communicate what he presents as private thoughts and sensations. In his famous private language argument, Wittgenstein argues that it would be impossible for this lone thinker to come up with ways to describe his subjective experiences to himself alone by making up a private language.[2] A philosophy based on introspection is impossible because a private language is impossible. Instead, Wittgenstein believed that philosophy's primary focus should be on language as an activity taking place among a community of language users.

Heidegger, on the other hand, rejects Cartesian mind–body dualism by showing thought to presuppose a relation to the world that comes before thinking.[3] In order to become a solitary thinker, one needs already to have been involved in practical tasks that do not involve a strict distinction between oneself and the world. Think, for example, of how a hammer works. When using the hammer successfully, it becomes an extension of your hand. If you start thinking about what you're doing, you will probably make a mistake. Heidegger thinks that it is only when the hammer breaks down that you need to start thinking about it as an object distinct from yourself, composed of parts, which can be put together in such-and-such a way so as to fix it. To see the hammer as an object, making the Cartesian distinction between self and world, you need to have been using the hammer as an extension of your body, in which case the Cartesian distinction is inapplicable.

Wittgenstein influenced the British philosopher Gilbert Ryle's* thought. It appears that Heidegger did as well, though this contention remains more controversial. In his book *The Concept of Mind*, Ryle offers some of the most influential twentieth-century criticism of Cartesian dualism.[4] He argues that our distinction between concepts pertaining to the mind and others pertaining to matter arise from a problematic use of language (and particularly through what he calls "category mistakes"). Ryle uses the catchphrase "the Ghost in the machine" to name what he takes to be "Descartes's myth" of the separation between mind and body.

Although still in many ways influential, Ryle's critique of Descartes (as well as Wittgenstein's, though to a lesser degree) came to be connected to a behavioristic* outlook (an approach to the theory of mind that emphasized the study of behavior as evidence of mental processes).

Contemporary philosophy of mind has largely abandoned behaviorism. Ryle's critique was, as Ryle himself explained, motivated by his desire to put to work the tools that had been developed by analytic philosophers in their investigation of language. Ironically, Ryle's text would invigorate philosophers' interest in the philosophy of mind. It was this interest that brought Descartes's ideas back to the foreground of philosophical discussion.

NOTES

1   Frank Jackson, "Epiphenomenal Qualia," *Philosophical Quarterly* 32, no. 127 (1982): 127–36.

2   See Ludwig Wittgenstein, *Philosophical Investigations*, trans. G. E. M. Anscombe (Oxford: Blackwell, 1953), 244–71. For an introduction to the argument, see Stewart Candlish and George Wrisley, "Private Language," in *The Stanford Encyclopedia of Philosophy* (Summer 2012), ed. E. N. Zalta, accessed July 26, 2015, http://plato.stanford.edu/archives/sum2012/entries/private-language/.

3   See, for example, Hubert Dreyfus, *Being-in-the-World: A Commentary on Heidegger's* Being and Time, *Division I* (Cambridge, MA: MIT Press, 1991).

4   Gilbert Ryle, *The Concept of Mind* (London: Hutchinson, 1949).

WHERE NEXT?

KEY POINTS

- Even though many of the doctrines it puts forth may simply be wrong, Descartes's *Meditations* will remain a classic text for anyone wishing to discuss the philosophy of mind.

- With the development of new technology and artificial intelligence, questions about the nature of consciousness become newly relevant. Reading Descartes shows how our ideas about the mind have evolved.

- Descartes's thought played a crucial role in rejecting the dogmatism* of the scholastics,* and inaugurated a modern way of debating ideas in philosophy.

Potential

Many twentieth-century philosophers hold views that were first held by Descartes. But it would be hard to speak of him as having modern "disciples." In other words, no particular school of philosophers holds the same views as those held by the Cartesians* of the early modern period* (roughly, the early 1500s to the late 1700s).

Descartes's thought will continue to be relevant to at least one aspect of contemporary scientific endeavor. As we learn more about how the brain functions, the question of the relation of the brain to consciousness becomes more crucial. Can our understanding of the brain lead to knowledge about the mind? Like various contemporary philosophers, Descartes would have answered no, since the brain and the mind are not the same kind of thing.

Given that Descartes was not informed by today's scientific

> **❝** Now, as more and more of our perception becomes indirect, read off various sorts of distance sensors and then presented by means of various sorts of displays, we are coming to realize how much of our knowledge is based on inferences that go beyond the evidence displayed on our screens. We see that the reality mediated by this tele-technology [cellular phones, teleconferencing, telecommuting, home shopping, telerobotics, and Internet web cameras] can always be called into question. Indeed, skepticism is increasingly reasonable in the face of the growing variety of illusions and tele-experiences now available. **❞**
>
> Hubert Dreyfus, "Telepistemology: Descartes's Last Stand"

advances, details of his views about the separation between mind and body may seem unrefined. But reworkings of Cartesian dualism still play a significant role in today's debates. Various contemporary philosophers have employed some intriguing thought experiments to defend versions of Cartesian mind–body dualism.*

However, there is a difference between Descartes's original formulation of dualism and contemporary defenses of it. Descartes had intended dualism to limit the domain of physics to matter, to advance the cause of "mechanical philosophy." Modern-day applications of dualism seem to seek to place checks and limitations on what science may come to know about the mind.

Future Directions

One intriguing thought experiment can be found in American philosopher Thomas Nagel's* 1974 paper "What Is It Like to Be a Bat?" Nagel imagines someone who knows all the objective facts about bats—for example, what they eat, what they can and cannot see, how they use sound to navigate, and so on. But can he know, through such a description, *what it is like* to be a bat? Cartesian dualists would say that he cannot. For a Cartesian dualist, an understanding of consciousness is like the subjective understanding of what it is like to be a bat.

The main question that Nagel's thought experiment raises was already on Descartes's mind when he made a distinction between knowledge of the material world (*res extensa**) and knowledge of the mind (*res cogitans**). Descartes was in effect asking how far science can go in explaining the world, including our minds. What happens, for example, when we begin studying the human brain, which seems to be the organ that allows us to undertake this study in the first place?

Of course, Descartes's own studies of the human brain did not help him find a plausible answer to the question of the interaction between mind and body. And though subsequent generations of thinkers have come up with some interesting theories, most of their answers have been found wanting by contemporary philosophy. As long as we attempt to comprehend this subject, we will be indebted to Descartes for posing it.

Summary
René Descartes's *Meditations on First Philosophy* remains an indispensable part of the canon of Western philosophy. No education in the humanities or liberal arts can be complete without engaging with *Meditations*, the ideas it expresses, and its overall approach to philosophical inquiry. Descartes's reflections on certainty and the dispelling of skeptical doubt, on the nature of the self, the mind, and the body are not simply crucial steps taken in the history of philosophy. Rather, they remain to this day constitutive of some of the most significant, interesting, and difficult questions human beings must ask of themselves.

A famous portrait of Descartes depicts him with one foot on a volume of Aristotle's* *Metaphysics*. While Aristotle shaped ancient philosophy, in many ways Descartes's work, and *Meditations* in particular, shaped what we now call modern philosophy. Over three and a half centuries after its publication, philosophers still work on problems first expressed by Descartes in the text. Our current and future efforts to understand consciousness are sure to keep *Meditations* relevant for generations to come. Not only a classic in the philosophical canon, Descartes's *Meditations* also remains a vibrant source of new ideas.

Unlike many of the canonical works in the history of modern philosophy, *Meditations* does not address itself only to specialists, or generally to intellectuals, but to all rational human beings. If, upon introspection, you find yourself capable of identifying the phenomena Descartes describes, then you are capable of negotiating, alongside Descartes's narrator, the ideas with which he struggles. Together with Descartes, anyone can look in her or himself, in meditation, and seek to find what Descartes also seeks: that is to say, the indubitable truth.

GLOSSARIES

GLOSSARY OF TERMS

Ancient skepticism: an ancient school of thought. There were two dominant schools of skepticism in antiquity: the milder academic skeptics (who traced their lineage back to Plato) and the Pyrrhonian skeptics. The latter are known for their spiritual exercise of *epoché*, a suspension of judgment regarding the truth or falsity of any belief that cannot be proven without doubt to be either true or false.

Behaviorism: an approach to psychology that avoids talking about private "mental states," shifting the emphasis instead toward studying outward behavior.

British empiricism: a movement—commonly opposed to continental rationalism—in seventeenth- and eighteenth-century philosophy, characterized by the thesis that experience is the sole source of knowledge. Among its leading proponents were John Locke, George Berkeley, and David Hume. The ideas of this historical movement are influential to this day.

Cartesian: relating to Descartes. In Descartes's time, academic treatises were written in Latin, and their authors commonly Latinized their names. The French Descartes becomes the Latin Cartesius, and so Descartes's followers are referred to as Cartesians.

Cartesian circle: a potential mistake in reasoning attributed to Descartes. The alleged mistake is that he thinks he argues that clear and distinct ideas are reliable because God cannot be a deceiver. But the existence of God is proven by Descartes on the basis that he has a clear and distinct idea of God. The circularity is that he assumes what he intends to prove, namely the reliability of clear and distinct ideas.

Cartesian coordinate system: the well-known way of specifying points on a two-axis plane.

Cognitive science: the science of intelligence, or cognition—an examination of the cognitive processes that occur as we acquire and make use of knowledge.

Continental rationalism: the philosophical tradition to which historians of philosophy have traditionally seen Descartes's work as belonging. The rationalists are generally characterized by their adherence to the idea that innate ideas exist. Apart from Descartes, Spinoza and Leibniz are generally thought to be leading proponents of rationalism.

Corpuscle: a small body or particle. In biology the term can refer to a cell or other small body. In physics it refers to the smallest constituent of matter or light. Descartes uses the term in the latter sense.

Dogmatism: the acceptance of certain teachings or philosophical positions as true without question.

Dualism: any system that explains a phenomenon with two separate and opposing principles. Mind–body dualism means that the mind and body are two separate and opposed things.

Early modern age: a period in history. Historians disagree as to exactly when this period begins: It is generally thought to start in the fifteenth or sixteenth century and end with the French Revolution. The period was already underway when Descartes was born.

Empiricism: approach in epistemology according to which truth can be arrived at only by means of sensory experience.

Epistemology: a branch of philosophy concerned with the nature and scope of knowledge. It examines what knowledge is, how it can be acquired, and how we can know when we have it.

Epoché: an ancient Greek word that translates as "suspension." In philosophy it describes the moment where all beliefs about the world are suspended, that is, when they are neither affirmed nor rejected.

Existentialist: roughly, a philosophical approach founded on the individual as capable of thought and action.

Foundationalism: refers to a claim about the justification of knowledge. The foundationalist view is that all knowledge is based on justified beliefs not inferred from further claims; these provide the foundation for all other knowledge.

Heretic: someone who challenges the authority and doctrines of an established religion.

Idealism: an eighteenth- and nineteenth-century German philosophical movement, with Johann Gottlieb Fichte, Friedrich Schelling, and Georg Wilhelm Friedrich Hegel its most famous proponents. The movement was a response to Kant's *Critique of Pure Reason* (1781). Kant thought that things as they are in themselves, independent of our thoughts and perceptions about them, cannot be known. German idealists, by contrast, thought that the nature of material things corresponds to the structure of our thought, leaving nothing unknowable. In other words, German idealists reject the opposition between thought and a reality outside of us.

Innate ideas: ideas that are not acquired through experience but are, rather, born with us.

Jesuits: members of the Society of Jesus, originating in the mid-sixteenth century. The society is a male congregation of the Catholic Church, now active in over a hundred countries around the world. They are involved in education, research, and charity work, and seek to foster dialogues among various Christian religious groups.

Metaphysics: a branch of philosophy concerned with explaining the nature of being. It considers both what there is and what it is like. It attempts to clarify fundamental notions such as space and time, objects and properties, cause and effect, and possibilities.

Ontological argument: an argument for the existence of God first introduced by the medieval theologian Anselm in his *Proslogion*. The argument, put simply, is that the definition of God implies that God must necessarily exist. If God is a perfect being then He must exist, for otherwise He would not have been perfect.

Ontology: the part of philosophy that deals with questions regarding being—that is, what kinds of things, broadly speaking, there are, or exist, or what reality is made of.

Parlement of Brittany: a court of justice in France, located in Rennes. It was active from the sixteenth to the eighteenth century.

Phenomenology: influential twentieth- and twenty-first-century philosophical tradition. Leading figures other than Edmund Husserl include the German philosopher Martin Heidegger, the French philosopher Maurice Merleau-Ponty, and the French existentialist philosopher Jean-Paul Sartre.

Plenum: refers to an enclosed space that is completely full. Descartes uses the term in his account of there being no vacuum or unfilled space in the extended world.

Port-Royal Grammar: work co-authored by the monk and grammarian Claude Lancelot and Antoine Arnauld. It was an important work in the philosophy of language and a stepping stone toward the development of modern linguistics.

Pyrrhonian skepticism: an ancient Greek school of skepticism founded by Aenesidemus in the first century B.C.E. The originator of ancient skepticism was Pyrrho of Elis and so the school was named after him. The central ideas of the school were written down by Sextus Empiricus in the second century C.E. Pyrrhonian skeptics suspend belief when something cannot be known with certainty. Their skepticism is therefore a result of inquiry rather than dismissing the possibility for acquiring true belief from the start.

Rationalism: an approach in epistemology according to which truth can be arrived at only—or chiefly—through reasoning, rather than via sensory experience. Rationalists typically think that knowledge can be deduced from basic principles.

Renaissance: a period in European history from the fourteenth until the seventeenth century, bridging the Middle Ages and modern history. It started in Italy as a cultural, intellectual, and artistic revival of ancient Greek and Roman culture. The word means literally "rebirth."

Res cogitans: a Latin term that translates as "thinking thing" or "mental thing." The term was used by Descartes, who thought the world consists of two substances: a mental and a physical substance. "*Res cogitans*" refers to the former.

Res extensa*:* a Latin term that translates as "extended thing." The term was used by Descartes, who thought that one of the two substances (mental substance, or *res cogitans,* being the other one) could best be defined as extension.

Scholasticism: the Aristotelian philosophical tradition dominant in medieval universities, founded around the eleventh century predominantly through the writings of Thomas Aquinas. Aquinas had reinterpreted and expanded Aristotle's work in a way that was seen as compatible with Christian dogma.

Skepticism: a questioning attitude to one's beliefs, or a general sense of doubt regarding claims that are generally taken for granted.

Sorbonne: Sorbonne College was the first college in Paris, founded in 1257. Currently the Sorbonne houses various Parisian universities, including the Paris-Sorbonne, the École nationale des chartes, and the École pratique des hautes études.

***Telos*:** the ancient Greek word for purpose or goal. The term is commonly associated with Aristotle's metaphysics, as Aristotle thought any object has an intrinsic purpose or goal. Moreover, Aristotle held that any object could best be defined by this purpose or goal. So the purpose of a knife is to cut, and the definition of a knife is something like a cutting thing.

Universal grammar: theory in linguistics generally attributed to Noam Chomsky. The theory states that the ability to learn a language is innate and fixed in our brains. As a result, it holds that all languages in the world must share certain features. These shared features are referred to as universal grammar.

PEOPLE MENTIONED IN THE TEXT

Anselm (1033–1109), Archbishop of Canterbury and Roman Catholic saint, was a philosopher and theologian. He is famous for putting forth an attempted proof of the existence of God known as the "ontological argument."

Thomas Aquinas (1225–74) was an Italian Catholic priest who was immensely influential as a philosopher and theologian. He adopted many of Aristotle's views and tried to make them cohere with central tenets of the Bible. The resulting philosophy is called "Thomism" and is contained in his most famous work, *Summa Theologica.*

Archimedes (c. 287–c. 212 B.C.E.) was a Syracusan mathematician, natural philosopher, engineer, and inventor. He famously said that he could move the entire earth if only he had a lever, a place to stand, and an unshakably solid point.

Aristarchus of Samos (310–230 B.C.E.) was an ancient Greek astronomer and mathematician who presented the first model of the universe with the sun at the center and the earth revolving around it.

Aristotle (384–322 B.C.E.) was a classical Greek philosopher and a student of Plato. His ideas helped shape Western philosophy and history. His work covers subjects including linguistics, physics, poetry, music, biology, politics, and ethics.

Antoine Arnauld (1612–94) was a French priest, theologian, philosopher, and mathematician. In 1660 he co-authored the *Port-Royal Grammar*, an important work in the philosophy of language and a stepping stone in the development of modern linguistics.

Augustine of Hippo (354–430 C.E.) was one of the major Western Christian philosophers and theologians. He exercised a formative influence on the Roman Catholic Church, which considers him a saint, and his *Confessions* is one of the first known works of autobiography.

Marcus Aurelius Antoninus Augustus (121–180 C.E.) was not only an emperor of Rome but also an important Stoic philosopher. Written while on campaign, his *Meditations* was a personal diary, apparently not meant for publication, recording his thoughts and generally Stoic outlook on life.

Isaac Beeckman (1588–1637) was a Dutch natural philosopher. Although he did not publish any of his work, he is considered to have been influential on contemporary scientists, including the young Descartes. His journals show him to have been among the first modern scientists to adopt atomism.

George Berkeley (1685–1753) was an Irish Catholic bishop and one of the leading figures of British empiricism. Berkeley is known for his version of idealism, which denies the existence of the material world. Among his greatest works are *A Treatise Concerning the Principles of Human Knowledge* (1710) and *Three Dialogues between Hylas and Philonous* (1713).

Pierre Bourdin (1595–1653) was a French philosopher and Jesuit priest, whose objection to *Meditations* related to the nature of consciousness.

Johannes Caterus (1590–1655) was a Dutch theologian and the author of the first set of objections to Descartes's *Meditations*, concerning his proof for the existence of God.

Noam Chomsky (b. 1928) is an American linguist and public intellectual. He is among the most influential academics of the twentieth century. His work in linguistics is partly responsible for the development of the field into a science, while he is famous for his political commentary, which includes a critique of US foreign policy.

Nicolaus Copernicus (1473–1543) was a famous Polish mathematician and astronomer. He proposed a heliocentric view of the cosmos—the view that the sun was at the center of the solar system.

Géraud de Cordemoy (1626–84) was a French lawyer and Cartesian philosopher who made some important contributions to contemporary philosophy of language. His most influential work on language, *Discours physique de la parole* (1668), was parodied in Molière's comic play and ballet *Le Bourgeois gentilhomme* (1670).

Princess Elisabeth of Bohemia (1618–80) was the daughter of Frederick V, Elector Palatine (nicknamed the Winter King for being king of Bohemia during only one winter). Her education developed an interest in philosophy, which in turn led to her correspondence with Descartes. She was later also in contact with the philosopher Gottfried Wilhelm Leibniz.

Sextus Empiricus (160–210 c.e.) was an ancient philosopher of the Pyrrhonian skeptic school. Among his writings we find accounts of the skeptical exercise of *epoché*, a suspension of judgment regarding the truth or falsity of any belief that cannot be proven without doubt to be either true or false.

Galileo Galilei (1564–1642) was a Florentine philosopher, mathematician, physicist, and astronomer. He is considered to be the founder of modern science and his magnum opus, *Dialogue Concerning the Two Chief World Systems* (1632), debated whether the sun or the earth is at the center of the solar system.

Pierre Gassendi (1592–1655) was a French priest, natural philosopher, scholar, and mathematician. He is well known for his defense of atomism in physics and was a proponent of skepticism, which informed his subsequent disagreement with Descartes over the method through which certain knowledge may be achieved.

Georg Wilhelm Friedrich Hegel (1770–1831) was among the most important German philosophers after Kant. His major works include *Phenomenology of Spirit* (1807) and *The Science of Logic* (1812–16).

Martin Heidegger (1889–1976) was a controversial German philosopher. His magnum opus, titled *Being and Time* (1927) and dedicated to his teacher Edmund Husserl, is thought to be one of the central works of the phenomenological movement. It has been interpreted as containing a critique of the Cartesian emphasis on consciousness.

Thomas Hobbes (1588–1679) was an English philosopher, mathematician, historian, and theologian. He is to this day considered one of the founding figures in modern political philosophy, which he explores in his magnum opus, *Leviathan* (1651).

Friedrich Wilhelm Christian Karl Ferdinand von Humboldt (1767–1835) was a Prussian philosopher whose contributions to linguistics were influential in the development of the field.

David Hume (1711–76) was a Scottish philosopher, the last of the three great British empiricists. Hume's philosophy is a form of empiricist skepticism developed first in *A Treatise of Human Nature* (1739), and subsequently in *An Enquiry Concerning Human Understanding* (1748), as well as in other works.

Edmund Husserl (1859–1938) was a German (Moravian) philosopher, known as the founder of twentieth-century phenomenology, or the examination of the structures of consciousness.

Frank Jackson (b. 1943) is an Australian philosopher. He is among the key contributors to contemporary debates on the nature of mind. Though famous for his thought experiment in favor of a kind of dualism, he subsequently rejected dualist views in the philosophy of mind in favor of "physicalism."

Immanuel Kant (1724–1804) was a German (Prussian) philosopher who questioned the path that Descartes had paved for philosophy. In his *Critique of Pure Reason* (1781), his stated goal is to solve the problem of the existence of the external world, by changing the way Descartes had formulated it.

Gottfried Wilhelm Leibniz (1646–1716) was a philosopher and polymath who followed in Descartes's and Spinoza's footsteps in accepting the existence of innate ideas. Among his most famous works is his posthumously published *Monadologie*, written in 1714, which includes an elaborate solution to the Cartesian problem of the interaction between mind and body.

John Locke (1632–1704) was an English philosopher and founder of the British empiricist tradition. At the core of empiricism is the idea, put forth by Locke, that an individual is born a *tabula rasa* (as a "blank slate"), and thus rejects the opposing rationalist doctrine of our having innate ideas. He developed this idea in his *Essay Concerning Human Understanding* (1690).

Maurice of Nassau (1567–1625) was Prince of Orange and head of state ("*stadtholder*") of the United Provinces of the Netherlands (1585–1625). He was a strategist and made significant reforms in the military training of the Dutch army. It is speculated that Descartes's position in Maurice's army was related to education in the military academies in Breda (see Tom Sorell's 1987 text, *Descartes: A Very Short Introduction*, 6).

Marin Mersenne (1588–1648) was a French Jesuit theologian, philosopher, and mathematician. He was acquainted with some of the leading figures in the development of science at the time, and it was through him that Descartes came in contact with them. He was also among the most important music theorists of his era.

Michel de Montaigne (1533–92) was a French Renaissance philosopher. His *Essais*, first published in 1580, is a collection of short philosophical writings on a vast range of different subjects. Montaigne's work is informed by his reading of the works of Sextus Empiricus, an ancient philosopher of the skeptic school.

Thomas Nagel (b. 1937) is an American philosopher based at New York University. His most important work has been in the philosophy of mind, ethics, and political philosophy. His best-known books are *The View From Nowhere* (1986) and *Mortal Questions* (1991).

87

Hilary Putnam (b. 1926) is an important figure in contemporary analytic philosophy. He has made significant contributions to discussions of the philosophy of mind and language. He is also well known for having produced some widely discussed thought experiments, including the brain-in-a-vat hypothesis.

Henricus Regius (1598–1679) was a Dutch philosopher and physician who worked at Utrecht University. Although mainly known due to his correspondence with Descartes, he is also the author of a book on natural philosophy, *Fundamenta Physices* (1646).

Bertrand Russell (1872–1970) was a well-known British philosopher, logician, mathematician, historian, and political activist. He is considered a founder of analytic philosophy and is the author, along with A. N. Whitehead, of *Principia Mathematica* (1910–13).

Gilbert Ryle (1900–76) was a British analytic philosopher and an important figure in the development of philosophy in Oxford during the 1940s and 1950s.

Jean-Paul Sartre (1905–80) was a prominent French philosopher, novelist, dramatist, public intellectual, and Marxist activist. Influenced by Husserl and Heidegger, Sartre developed, in *Being and Nothingness* (1943), what is called "existentialist" philosophy, which became known internationally after World War II.

Baruch Spinoza (1632–77) was a leading Dutch philosopher. His questioning of religious beliefs made him a controversial figure in the early modern world. One of his earliest writings was the *Principia Philosophiae Cartesianae* (1663), an exposition of Descartes's views. Spinoza followed Descartes in thinking that innate ideas exist. In his *Ethics*, published posthumously in 1677, he rejected

Descartes's substance dualism in favor of monism: the idea that there is only one kind of substance.

Gisbert Voetius (1589–1976) was a Dutch Calvinist theologian, working as the rector of Utrecht University. He is mainly known for his condemnation of Descartes's ideas.

Ludwig Wittgenstein (1889–1951) is considered to be among the leading twentieth-century philosophers. In his posthumously published *Philosophical Investigations* (1953) he criticizes the focus of philosophy on the private individual, which is largely due to Descartes.

WORKS CITED

WORKS CITED

Anselm, St., Archbishop of Canterbury. *Monologion and Proslogion: With the Replies of Gaunilo and Anselm.* Translated, with introduction and notes, by Thomas Williams. Indianapolis: Hackett Publishing, 1996.

Bolyard, C. "Medieval Skepticism." In *The Stanford Encyclopedia of Philosophy* (Spring 2013), edited by E. N. Zalta. Accessed July 27, 2015. http://plato.stanford.edu/archives/spr2013/entries/skepticism-medieval/.

Candlish, Stewart, and George Wrisley. "Private Language." In *The Stanford Encyclopedia of Philosophy* (Summer 2012), edited by E. N. Zalta. Accessed July 27, 2015. http://plato.stanford.edu/archives/sum2012/entries/private-language/.

Chomsky, Noam. *Cartesian Linguistics: A Chapter in the History of Rationalist Thought.* New York: Harper & Row, 1966.

Cottingham, John. "Cartesian Dualism: Theology, Metaphysics, and Science." In *The Cambridge Companion to Descartes*, edited by John Cottingham, 236–57. Cambridge: Cambridge University Press, 1992.

Descartes, René. *Musicae Compendium.* Amsterdam: Joannem Janssonium Juniorem, 1656.

―――. *Discourse on Method, Optics, Geometry and Meteorology.* Translated by Paul J. Olscamp. Indianapolis, IN: Bobbs-Merrill, 1965.

―――. *Le Monde, ou Traité de la lumière.* Translated and with an introduction by Michael Sean Mahoney. New York: Abaris Books, 1979.

―――. *Principles of Philosophy.* Translated by V. R. Miller and R. P. Miller. Dordrecht: D. Reidel, 1983.

―――. *The Passions of the Soul.* Translated by Stephen H. Voss. Indianapolis, IN: Hackett Publishing, 1989.

―――. *Meditations on First Philosophy: With Selections from the Objections and Replies.* Edited and translated by John Cottingham. Cambridge: Cambridge University Press, 1996.

Dretske, Fred. "Doubts about *Cogito.*" *Grazer Philosophische Studien* 84, no.1 (2012): 1–17.

Dreyfus, Hubert. *Being-in-the-World: A Commentary on Heidegger's* Being and Time*, Division I.* Cambridge, MA: MIT Press, 1991.

―――. "Telepistemology: Descartes's Last Stand." In *The Robot in the Garden*, edited by Ken Goldberg. Cambridge, MA: MIT Press, 2000.

Elisabeth, Princess of Bohemia, and René Descartes. *The Correspondence Between Princess Elisabeth of Bohemia and René Descartes*. Edited and translated by Lisa Shapiro. Chicago: University of Chicago Press, 2007.

Hill, James. "Meditating with Descartes." *Richmond Journal of Philosophy* 12 (2006).

Hume, David. *An Enquiry Concerning Human Understanding and Other Writings.* Edited by Stephen Buckle. Cambridge: Cambridge University Press, 2007.

Jackson, Frank. "Epiphenomenal Qualia." *Philosophical Quarterly* 32, no. 127 (1982): 127–36.

Montaigne, Michel de. *The Complete Essays of Montaigne*. Translated by Donald Frame. Stanford, CA: Stanford University Press, 1957.

Nolan, Lawrence. "Descartes's Ontological Argument." In *The Stanford Encyclopedia of Philosophy* (Summer 2011), edited by E. N. Zalta. Accessed September 10, 2013. http://plato.stanford.edu/archives/sum2011/entries/descartes-ontological/.

Pereboom, Derk. "Kant's Transcendental Arguments." In *The Stanford Encyclopedia of Philosophy* (Winter 2009), edited by E. N. Zalta. Accessed July 26, 2015. http://plato.stanford.edu/archives/win2009/entries/kant-transcendental/.

Putnam, Hilary. *Reason, Truth and History*. Cambridge: Cambridge University Press, 1981.

Rée, Jonathan. *Descartes*. London: Allen Lane, 1974.

— — —. *Philosophical Tales: An Essay on Philosophy and Literature*. New York: Methuen, 1987.

Rorty, Richard. *Philosophy and the Mirror of Nature*. Princeton, NJ: Princeton University Press, 2009.

Russell, Bertrand. *History of Western Philosophy*. Oxon, UK: Routledge, 2004.

Ryle, Gilbert. *The Concept of Mind*. London: Hutchinson, 1949.

Smith, Kurt. "Descartes's Life and Works." In *The Stanford Encyclopedia of Philosophy* (Fall 2012), edited by E. N. Zalta. Accessed July 27, 2015. http://plato.stanford.edu/archives/fall2012/entries/descartes-works/.

Sorell, Tom. *Descartes: A Very Short Introduction.* Oxford: Oxford University Press, 1987.

Wittgenstein, Ludwig. *Philosophical Investigations*. Translated by G. E. M. Anscombe. Oxford: Blackwell, 1953.

THE MACAT LIBRARY
BY DISCIPLINE

The Macat Library By Discipline

AFRICANA STUDIES

Chinua Achebe's *An Image of Africa: Racism in Conrad's Heart of Darkness*
W. E. B. Du Bois's *The Souls of Black Folk*
Zora Neale Huston's *Characteristics of Negro Expression*
Martin Luther King Jr's *Why We Can't Wait*
Toni Morrison's *Playing in the Dark: Whiteness in the American Literary Imagination*

ANTHROPOLOGY

Arjun Appadurai's *Modernity at Large: Cultural Dimensions of Globalisation*
Philippe Ariès's *Centuries of Childhood*
Franz Boas's *Race, Language and Culture*
Kim Chan & Renée Mauborgne's *Blue Ocean Strategy*
Jared Diamond's *Guns, Germs & Steel: the Fate of Human Societies*
Jared Diamond's *Collapse: How Societies Choose to Fail or Survive*
E. E. Evans-Pritchard's *Witchcraft, Oracles and Magic Among the Azande*
James Ferguson's *The Anti-Politics Machine*
Clifford Geertz's *The Interpretation of Cultures*
David Graeber's *Debt: the First 5000 Years*
Karen Ho's *Liquidated: An Ethnography of Wall Street*
Geert Hofstede's *Culture's Consequences: Comparing Values, Behaviors, Institutes and Organizations across Nations*
Claude Lévi-Strauss's *Structural Anthropology*
Jay Macleod's *Ain't No Makin' It: Aspirations and Attainment in a Low-Income Neighborhood*
Saba Mahmood's *The Politics of Piety: The Islamic Revival and the Feminist Subject*
Marcel Mauss's *The Gift*

BUSINESS

Jean Lave & Etienne Wenger's *Situated Learning*
Theodore Levitt's *Marketing Myopia*
Burton G. Malkiel's *A Random Walk Down Wall Street*
Douglas McGregor's *The Human Side of Enterprise*
Michael Porter's *Competitive Strategy: Creating and Sustaining Superior Performance*
John Kotter's *Leading Change*
C. K. Prahalad & Gary Hamel's *The Core Competence of the Corporation*

CRIMINOLOGY

Michelle Alexander's *The New Jim Crow: Mass Incarceration in the Age of Colorblindness*
Michael R. Gottfredson & Travis Hirschi's *A General Theory of Crime*
Richard Herrnstein & Charles A. Murray's *The Bell Curve: Intelligence and Class Structure in American Life*
Elizabeth Loftus's *Eyewitness Testimony*
Jay Macleod's *Ain't No Makin' It: Aspirations and Attainment in a Low-Income Neighborhood*
Philip Zimbardo's *The Lucifer Effect*

ECONOMICS

Janet Abu-Lughod's *Before European Hegemony*
Ha-Joon Chang's *Kicking Away the Ladder*
David Brion Davis's *The Problem of Slavery in the Age of Revolution*
Milton Friedman's *The Role of Monetary Policy*
Milton Friedman's *Capitalism and Freedom*
David Graeber's *Debt: the First 5000 Years*
Friedrich Hayek's *The Road to Serfdom*
Karen Ho's *Liquidated: An Ethnography of Wall Street*

John Maynard Keynes's *The General Theory of Employment, Interest and Money*
Charles P. Kindleberger's *Manias, Panics and Crashes*
Robert Lucas's *Why Doesn't Capital Flow from Rich to Poor Countries?*
Burton G. Malkiel's *A Random Walk Down Wall Street*
Thomas Robert Malthus's *An Essay on the Principle of Population*
Karl Marx's *Capital*
Thomas Piketty's *Capital in the Twenty-First Century*
Amartya Sen's *Development as Freedom*
Adam Smith's *The Wealth of Nations*
Nassim Nicholas Taleb's *The Black Swan: The Impact of the Highly Improbable*
Amos Tversky's & Daniel Kahneman's *Judgment under Uncertainty: Heuristics and Biases*
Mahbub Ul Haq's *Reflections on Human Development*
Max Weber's *The Protestant Ethic and the Spirit of Capitalism*

FEMINISM AND GENDER STUDIES

Judith Butler's *Gender Trouble*
Simone De Beauvoir's *The Second Sex*
Michel Foucault's *History of Sexuality*
Betty Friedan's *The Feminine Mystique*
Saba Mahmood's *The Politics of Piety: The Islamic Revival and the Feminist Subject*
Joan Wallach Scott's *Gender and the Politics of History*
Mary Wollstonecraft's *A Vindication of the Rights of Woman*
Virginia Woolf's *A Room of One's Own*

GEOGRAPHY

The Brundtland Report's *Our Common Future*
Rachel Carson's *Silent Spring*
Charles Darwin's *On the Origin of Species*
James Ferguson's *The Anti-Politics Machine*
Jane Jacobs's *The Death and Life of Great American Cities*
James Lovelock's *Gaia: A New Look at Life on Earth*
Amartya Sen's *Development as Freedom*
Mathis Wackernagel & William Rees's *Our Ecological Footprint*

HISTORY

Janet Abu-Lughod's *Before European Hegemony*
Benedict Anderson's *Imagined Communities*
Bernard Bailyn's *The Ideological Origins of the American Revolution*
Hanna Batatu's *The Old Social Classes And The Revolutionary Movements Of Iraq*
Christopher Browning's *Ordinary Men: Reserve Police Batallion 101 and the Final Solution in Poland*
Edmund Burke's *Reflections on the Revolution in France*
William Cronon's *Nature's Metropolis: Chicago And The Great West*
Alfred W. Crosby's *The Columbian Exchange*
Hamid Dabashi's *Iran: A People Interrupted*
David Brion Davis's *The Problem of Slavery in the Age of Revolution*
Nathalie Zemon Davis's *The Return of Martin Guerre*
Jared Diamond's *Guns, Germs & Steel: the Fate of Human Societies*
Frank Dikotter's *Mao's Great Famine*
John W Dower's *War Without Mercy: Race And Power In The Pacific War*
W. E. B. Du Bois's *The Souls of Black Folk*
Richard J. Evans's *In Defence of History*
Lucien Febvre's *The Problem of Unbelief in the 16th Century*
Sheila Fitzpatrick's *Everyday Stalinism*

The Macat Library By Discipline

Eric Foner's *Reconstruction: America's Unfinished Revolution, 1863-1877*
Michel Foucault's *Discipline and Punish*
Michel Foucault's *History of Sexuality*
Francis Fukuyama's *The End of History and the Last Man*
John Lewis Gaddis's *We Now Know: Rethinking Cold War History*
Ernest Gellner's *Nations and Nationalism*
Eugene Genovese's *Roll, Jordan, Roll: The World the Slaves Made*
Carlo Ginzburg's *The Night Battles*
Daniel Goldhagen's *Hitler's Willing Executioners*
Jack Goldstone's *Revolution and Rebellion in the Early Modern World*
Antonio Gramsci's *The Prison Notebooks*
Alexander Hamilton, John Jay & James Madison's *The Federalist Papers*
Christopher Hill's *The World Turned Upside Down*
Carole Hillenbrand's *The Crusades: Islamic Perspectives*
Thomas Hobbes's *Leviathan*
Eric Hobsbawm's *The Age Of Revolution*
John A. Hobson's *Imperialism: A Study*
Albert Hourani's *History of the Arab Peoples*
Samuel P. Huntington's *The Clash of Civilizations and the Remaking of World Order*
C. L. R. James's *The Black Jacobins*
Tony Judt's *Postwar: A History of Europe Since 1945*
Ernst Kantorowicz's *The King's Two Bodies: A Study in Medieval Political Theology*
Paul Kennedy's *The Rise and Fall of the Great Powers*
Ian Kershaw's *The "Hitler Myth": Image and Reality in the Third Reich*
John Maynard Keynes's *The General Theory of Employment, Interest and Money*
Charles P. Kindleberger's *Manias, Panics and Crashes*
Martin Luther King Jr's *Why We Can't Wait*
Henry Kissinger's *World Order: Reflections on the Character of Nations and the Course of History*
Thomas Kuhn's *The Structure of Scientific Revolutions*
Georges Lefebvre's *The Coming of the French Revolution*
John Locke's *Two Treatises of Government*
Niccolò Machiavelli's *The Prince*
Thomas Robert Malthus's *An Essay on the Principle of Population*
Mahmood Mamdani's *Citizen and Subject: Contemporary Africa And The Legacy Of Late Colonialism*
Karl Marx's *Capital*
Stanley Milgram's *Obedience to Authority*
John Stuart Mill's *On Liberty*
Thomas Paine's *Common Sense*
Thomas Paine's *Rights of Man*
Geoffrey Parker's *Global Crisis: War, Climate Change and Catastrophe in the Seventeenth Century*
Jonathan Riley-Smith's *The First Crusade and the Idea of Crusading*
Jean-Jacques Rousseau's *The Social Contract*
Joan Wallach Scott's *Gender and the Politics of History*
Theda Skocpol's *States and Social Revolutions*
Adam Smith's *The Wealth of Nations*
Timothy Snyder's *Bloodlands: Europe Between Hitler and Stalin*
Sun Tzu's *The Art of War*
Keith Thomas's *Religion and the Decline of Magic*
Thucydides's *The History of the Peloponnesian War*
Frederick Jackson Turner's *The Significance of the Frontier in American History*
Odd Arne Westad's *The Global Cold War: Third World Interventions And The Making Of Our Times*

LITERATURE

Chinua Achebe's *An Image of Africa: Racism in Conrad's Heart of Darkness*
Roland Barthes's *Mythologies*
Homi K. Bhabha's *The Location of Culture*
Judith Butler's *Gender Trouble*
Simone De Beauvoir's *The Second Sex*
Ferdinand De Saussure's *Course in General Linguistics*
T. S. Eliot's *The Sacred Wood: Essays on Poetry and Criticism*
Zora Neale Huston's *Characteristics of Negro Expression*
Toni Morrison's *Playing in the Dark: Whiteness in the American Literary Imagination*
Edward Said's *Orientalism*
Gayatri Chakravorty Spivak's *Can the Subaltern Speak?*
Mary Wollstonecraft's *A Vindication of the Rights of Women*
Virginia Woolf's *A Room of One's Own*

PHILOSOPHY

Elizabeth Anscombe's *Modern Moral Philosophy*
Hannah Arendt's *The Human Condition*
Aristotle's *Metaphysics*
Aristotle's *Nicomachean Ethics*
Edmund Gettier's *Is Justified True Belief Knowledge?*
Georg Wilhelm Friedrich Hegel's *Phenomenology of Spirit*
David Hume's *Dialogues Concerning Natural Religion*
David Hume's *The Enquiry for Human Understanding*
Immanuel Kant's *Religion within the Boundaries of Mere Reason*
Immanuel Kant's *Critique of Pure Reason*
Søren Kierkegaard's *The Sickness Unto Death*
Søren Kierkegaard's *Fear and Trembling*
C. S. Lewis's *The Abolition of Man*
Alasdair MacIntyre's *After Virtue*
Marcus Aurelius's *Meditations*
Friedrich Nietzsche's *On the Genealogy of Morality*
Friedrich Nietzsche's *Beyond Good and Evil*
Plato's *Republic*
Plato's *Symposium*
Jean-Jacques Rousseau's *The Social Contract*
Gilbert Ryle's *The Concept of Mind*
Baruch Spinoza's *Ethics*
Sun Tzu's *The Art of War*
Ludwig Wittgenstein's *Philosophical Investigations*

POLITICS

Benedict Anderson's *Imagined Communities*
Aristotle's *Politics*
Bernard Bailyn's *The Ideological Origins of the American Revolution*
Edmund Burke's *Reflections on the Revolution in France*
John C. Calhoun's *A Disquisition on Government*
Ha-Joon Chang's *Kicking Away the Ladder*
Hamid Dabashi's *Iran: A People Interrupted*
Hamid Dabashi's *Theology of Discontent: The Ideological Foundation of the Islamic Revolution in Iran*
Robert Dahl's *Democracy and its Critics*
Robert Dahl's *Who Governs?*
David Brion Davis's *The Problem of Slavery in the Age of Revolution*

The Macat Library By Discipline

Alexis De Tocqueville's *Democracy in America*
James Ferguson's *The Anti-Politics Machine*
Frank Dikotter's *Mao's Great Famine*
Sheila Fitzpatrick's *Everyday Stalinism*
Eric Foner's *Reconstruction: America's Unfinished Revolution, 1863-1877*
Milton Friedman's *Capitalism and Freedom*
Francis Fukuyama's *The End of History and the Last Man*
John Lewis Gaddis's *We Now Know: Rethinking Cold War History*
Ernest Gellner's *Nations and Nationalism*
David Graeber's *Debt: the First 5000 Years*
Antonio Gramsci's *The Prison Notebooks*
Alexander Hamilton, John Jay & James Madison's *The Federalist Papers*
Friedrich Hayek's *The Road to Serfdom*
Christopher Hill's *The World Turned Upside Down*
Thomas Hobbes's *Leviathan*
John A. Hobson's *Imperialism: A Study*
Samuel P. Huntington's *The Clash of Civilizations and the Remaking of World Order*
Tony Judt's *Postwar: A History of Europe Since 1945*
David C. Kang's *China Rising: Peace, Power and Order in East Asia*
Paul Kennedy's *The Rise and Fall of Great Powers*
Robert Keohane's *After Hegemony*
Martin Luther King Jr.'s *Why We Can't Wait*
Henry Kissinger's *World Order: Reflections on the Character of Nations and the Course of History*
John Locke's *Two Treatises of Government*
Niccolò Machiavelli's *The Prince*
Thomas Robert Malthus's *An Essay on the Principle of Population*
Mahmood Mamdani's *Citizen and Subject: Contemporary Africa And The Legacy Of Late Colonialism*
Karl Marx's *Capital*
John Stuart Mill's *On Liberty*
John Stuart Mill's *Utilitarianism*
Hans Morgenthau's *Politics Among Nations*
Thomas Paine's *Common Sense*
Thomas Paine's *Rights of Man*
Thomas Piketty's *Capital in the Twenty-First Century*
Robert D. Putman's *Bowling Alone*
John Rawls's *Theory of Justice*
Jean-Jacques Rousseau's *The Social Contract*
Theda Skocpol's *States and Social Revolutions*
Adam Smith's *The Wealth of Nations*
Sun Tzu's *The Art of War*
Henry David Thoreau's *Civil Disobedience*
Thucydides's *The History of the Peloponnesian War*
Kenneth Waltz's *Theory of International Politics*
Max Weber's *Politics as a Vocation*
Odd Arne Westad's *The Global Cold War: Third World Interventions And The Making Of Our Times*

POSTCOLONIAL STUDIES

Roland Barthes's *Mythologies*
Frantz Fanon's *Black Skin, White Masks*
Homi K. Bhabha's *The Location of Culture*
Gustavo Gutiérrez's *A Theology of Liberation*
Edward Said's *Orientalism*
Gayatri Chakravorty Spivak's *Can the Subaltern Speak?*

PSYCHOLOGY

Gordon Allport's *The Nature of Prejudice*
Alan Baddeley & Graham Hitch's *Aggression: A Social Learning Analysis*
Albert Bandura's *Aggression: A Social Learning Analysis*
Leon Festinger's *A Theory of Cognitive Dissonance*
Sigmund Freud's *The Interpretation of Dreams*
Betty Friedan's *The Feminine Mystique*
Michael R. Gottfredson & Travis Hirschi's *A General Theory of Crime*
Eric Hoffer's *The True Believer: Thoughts on the Nature of Mass Movements*
William James's *Principles of Psychology*
Elizabeth Loftus's *Eyewitness Testimony*
A. H. Maslow's *A Theory of Human Motivation*
Stanley Milgram's *Obedience to Authority*
Steven Pinker's *The Better Angels of Our Nature*
Oliver Sacks's *The Man Who Mistook His Wife For a Hat*
Richard Thaler & Cass Sunstein's *Nudge: Improving Decisions About Health, Wealth and Happiness*
Amos Tversky's *Judgment under Uncertainty: Heuristics and Biases*
Philip Zimbardo's *The Lucifer Effect*

SCIENCE

Rachel Carson's *Silent Spring*
William Cronon's *Nature's Metropolis: Chicago And The Great West*
Alfred W. Crosby's *The Columbian Exchange*
Charles Darwin's *On the Origin of Species*
Richard Dawkin's *The Selfish Gene*
Thomas Kuhn's *The Structure of Scientific Revolutions*
Geoffrey Parker's *Global Crisis: War, Climate Change and Catastrophe in the Seventeenth Century*
Mathis Wackernagel & William Rees's *Our Ecological Footprint*

SOCIOLOGY

Michelle Alexander's *The New Jim Crow: Mass Incarceration in the Age of Colorblindness*
Gordon Allport's *The Nature of Prejudice*
Albert Bandura's *Aggression: A Social Learning Analysis*
Hanna Batatu's *The Old Social Classes And The Revolutionary Movements Of Iraq*
Ha-Joon Chang's *Kicking Away the Ladder*
W. E. B. Du Bois's *The Souls of Black Folk*
Émile Durkheim's *On Suicide*
Frantz Fanon's *Black Skin, White Masks*
Frantz Fanon's *The Wretched of the Earth*
Eric Foner's *Reconstruction: America's Unfinished Revolution, 1863-1877*
Eugene Genovese's *Roll, Jordan, Roll: The World the Slaves Made*
Jack Goldstone's *Revolution and Rebellion in the Early Modern World*
Antonio Gramsci's *The Prison Notebooks*
Richard Herrnstein & Charles A Murray's *The Bell Curve: Intelligence and Class Structure in American Life*
Eric Hoffer's *The True Believer: Thoughts on the Nature of Mass Movements*
Jane Jacobs's *The Death and Life of Great American Cities*
Robert Lucas's *Why Doesn't Capital Flow from Rich to Poor Countries?*
Jay Macleod's *Ain't No Makin' It: Aspirations and Attainment in a Low Income Neighborhood*
Elaine May's *Homeward Bound: American Families in the Cold War Era*
Douglas McGregor's *The Human Side of Enterprise*
C. Wright Mills's *The Sociological Imagination*

The Macat Library By Discipline

Thomas Piketty's *Capital in the Twenty-First Century*
Robert D. Putman's *Bowling Alone*
David Riesman's *The Lonely Crowd: A Study of the Changing American Character*
Edward Said's *Orientalism*
Joan Wallach Scott's *Gender and the Politics of History*
Theda Skocpol's *States and Social Revolutions*
Max Weber's *The Protestant Ethic and the Spirit of Capitalism*

THEOLOGY

Augustine's *Confessions*
Benedict's *Rule of St Benedict*
Gustavo Gutiérrez's *A Theology of Liberation*
Carole Hillenbrand's *The Crusades: Islamic Perspectives*
David Hume's *Dialogues Concerning Natural Religion*
Immanuel Kant's *Religion within the Boundaries of Mere Reason*
Ernst Kantorowicz's *The King's Two Bodies: A Study in Medieval Political Theology*
Søren Kierkegaard's *The Sickness Unto Death*
C. S. Lewis's *The Abolition of Man*
Saba Mahmood's *The Politics of Piety: The Islamic Revival and the Feminist Subject*
Baruch Spinoza's *Ethics*
Keith Thomas's *Religion and the Decline of Magic*

COMING SOON

Chris Argyris's *The Individual and the Organisation*
Seyla Benhabib's *The Rights of Others*
Walter Benjamin's *The Work Of Art in the Age of Mechanical Reproduction*
John Berger's *Ways of Seeing*
Pierre Bourdieu's *Outline of a Theory of Practice*
Mary Douglas's *Purity and Danger*
Roland Dworkin's *Taking Rights Seriously*
James G. March's *Exploration and Exploitation in Organisational Learning*
Ikujiro Nonaka's *A Dynamic Theory of Organizational Knowledge Creation*
Griselda Pollock's *Vision and Difference*
Amartya Sen's *Inequality Re-Examined*
Susan Sontag's *On Photography*
Yasser Tabbaa's *The Transformation of Islamic Art*
Ludwig von Mises's *Theory of Money and Credit*

The Macat Library By Discipline

Macat Disciplines

Access the greatest ideas and thinkers across entire disciplines, including

CRIMINOLOGY

Michelle Alexander's
The New Jim Crow: Mass Incarceration in the Age of Colorblindness

Michael R. Gottfredson & Travis Hirschi's
A General Theory of Crime

Elizabeth Loftus's
Eyewitness Testimony

Richard Herrnstein & Charles A. Murray's
The Bell Curve: Intelligence and Class Structure in American Life

Jay Macleod's
Ain't No Makin' It: Aspirations and Attainment in a Low-Income Neighborhood

Philip Zimbardo's
The Lucifer Effect

Macat analyses are available from all good bookshops and libraries.

Access hundreds of analyses through one, multimedia tool.
Join free for one month **library.macat.com**

Macat Disciplines

Access the greatest ideas and thinkers across entire disciplines, including

INEQUALITY

Ha-Joon Chang's, *Kicking Away the Ladder*

David Graeber's, *Debt: The First 5000 Years*

Robert E. Lucas's, *Why Doesn't Capital Flow from Rich To Poor Countries?*

Thomas Piketty's, *Capital in the Twenty-First Century*

Amartya Sen's, *Inequality Re-Examined*

Mahbub Ul Haq's, *Reflections on Human Development*

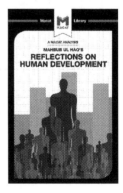

Macat Disciplines

Access the greatest ideas and thinkers across entire disciplines, including

MAN AND THE ENVIRONMENT

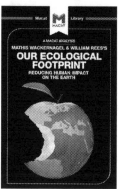

The Brundtland Report's, *Our Common Future*
Rachel Carson's, *Silent Spring*
James Lovelock's, *Gaia: A New Look at Life on Earth*
Mathis Wackernagel & William Rees's, *Our Ecological Footprint*

Macat analyses are available from all good bookshops and libraries.

Access hundreds of analyses through one, multimedia tool.
Join free for one month **library.macat.com**

Macat Disciplines

Access the greatest ideas and thinkers across entire disciplines, including

THE FUTURE OF DEMOCRACY

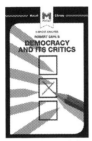

Robert A. Dahl's, *Democracy and Its Critics*
Robert A. Dahl's, *Who Governs?*
Alexis De Toqueville's, *Democracy in America*
Niccolò Machiavelli's, *The Prince*
John Stuart Mill's, *On Liberty*
Robert D. Putnam's, *Bowling Alone*
Jean-Jacques Rousseau's, *The Social Contract*
Henry David Thoreau's, *Civil Disobedience*

Macat Disciplines

Access the greatest ideas and thinkers across entire disciplines, including

TOTALITARIANISM

Sheila Fitzpatrick's, *Everyday Stalinism*
Ian Kershaw's, *The "Hitler Myth"*
Timothy Snyder's, *Bloodlands*

Macat analyses are available from all good bookshops and libraries.

Access hundreds of analyses through one, multimedia tool.
Join free for one month **library.macat.com**

Macat Pairs

Analyse historical and modern issues from opposite sides of an argument. Pairs include:

RACE AND IDENTITY

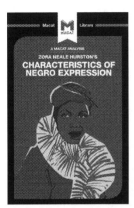

Zora Neale Hurston's
Characteristics of Negro Expression

Using material collected on anthropological expeditions to the South, Zora Neale Hurston explains how expression in African American culture in the early twentieth century departs from the art of white America. At the time, African American art was often criticized for copying white culture. For Hurston, this criticism misunderstood how art works. European tradition views art as something fixed. But Hurston describes a creative process that is alive, ever-changing, and largely improvisational. She maintains that African American art works through a process called 'mimicry'—where an imitated object or verbal pattern, for example, is reshaped and altered until it becomes something new, novel—and worthy of attention.

Frantz Fanon's
Black Skin, White Masks

Black Skin, White Masks offers a radical analysis of the psychological effects of colonization on the colonized.

Fanon witnessed the effects of colonization first hand both in his birthplace, Martinique, and again later in life when he worked as a psychiatrist in another French colony, Algeria. His text is uncompromising in form and argument. He dissects the dehumanizing effects of colonialism, arguing that it destroys the native sense of identity, forcing people to adapt to an alien set of values—including a core belief that they are inferior. This results in deep psychological trauma.

Fanon's work played a pivotal role in the civil rights movements of the 1960s.

Macat analyses are available from all good bookshops and libraries.

Access hundreds of analyses through one, multimedia tool.
Join free for one month **library.macat.com**

Macat Pairs

Analyse historical and modern issues from opposite sides of an argument. Pairs include:

INTERNATIONAL RELATIONS IN THE 21ST CENTURY

Samuel P. Huntington's
The Clash of Civilisations

In his highly influential 1996 book, Huntington offers a vision of a post-Cold War world in which conflict takes place not between competing ideologies but between cultures. The worst clash, he argues, will be between the Islamic world and the West: the West's arrogance and belief that its culture is a "gift" to the world will come into conflict with Islam's obstinacy and concern that its culture is under attack from a morally decadent "other."

Clash inspired much debate between different political schools of thought. But its greatest impact came in helping define American foreign policy in the wake of the 2001 terrorist attacks in New York and Washington.

Francis Fukuyama's
The End of History and the Last Man

Published in 1992, *The End of History and the Last Man* argues that capitalist democracy is the final destination for all societies. Fukuyama believed democracy triumphed during the Cold War because it lacks the "fundamental contradictions" inherent in communism and satisfies our yearning for freedom and equality. Democracy therefore marks the endpoint in the evolution of ideology, and so the "end of history." There will still be "events," but no fundamental change in ideology.

Macat Pairs

Analyse historical and modern issues from opposite sides of an argument. Pairs include:

HOW TO RUN AN ECONOMY

John Maynard Keynes's
The General Theory OF Employment, Interest and Money

Classical economics suggests that market economies are self-correcting in times of recession or depression, and tend toward full employment and output. But English economist John Maynard Keynes disagrees.

In his ground-breaking 1936 study *The General Theory*, Keynes argues that traditional economics has misunderstood the causes of unemployment. Employment is not determined by the price of labor; it is directly linked to demand. Keynes believes market economies are by nature unstable, and so require government intervention. Spurred on by the social catastrophe of the Great Depression of the 1930s, he sets out to revolutionize the way the world thinks

Milton Friedman's
The Role of Monetary Policy

Friedman's 1968 paper changed the course of economic theory. In just 17 pages, he demolished existing theory and outlined an effective alternate monetary policy designed to secure 'high employment, stable prices and rapid growth.'

Friedman demonstrated that monetary policy plays a vital role in broader economic stability and argued that economists got their monetary policy wrong in the 1950s and 1960s by misunderstanding the relationship between inflation and unemployment. Previous generations of economists had believed that governments could permanently decrease unemployment by permitting inflation—and vice versa. Friedman's most original contribution was to show that this supposed trade-off is an illusion that only works in the short term.

Macat analyses are available from all good bookshops and libraries.

Access hundreds of analyses through one, multimedia tool.
Join free for one month **library.macat.com**

Printed in the United States
by Baker & Taylor Publisher Services